Communications
in Computer and Information Science   460

T0224397

Takaya Yuizono   Gustavo Zurita
Nelson Baloian   Tomoo Inoue
Hiroaki Ogata (Eds.)

Collaboration Technologies and Social Computing

7th International Conference, CollabTech 2014
Santiago, Chile, September 8-10, 2014
Proceedings

Springer

Volume Editors

Takaya Yuizono
Japan Advanced Institute of Science and Technology
Ishikawa, Japan
E-mail: yuizono@jaist.ac.jp

Gustavo Zurita
Universidad de Chile, Santiago, Chile
E-mail: gzurita@fen.uchile.cl

Nelson Baloian
Universidad de Chile, Santiago, Chile
E-mail: nbaloian@gmail.com

Tomoo Inoue
University of Tsukuba, Japan
E-mail: inoue@slis.tsukuba.ac.jp

Hiroaki Ogata
Kyushu University, Fukuoka, Japan
E-mail: hiroaki.ogata@gmail.com

ISSN 1865-0929   e-ISSN 1865-0937
ISBN 978-3-662-44650-8   e-ISBN 978-3-662-44651-5
DOI 10.1007/978-3-662-44651-5
Springer Heidelberg New York Dordrecht London

Library of Congress Control Number: 2014946440

Typesetting: Camera-ready by author, data conversion by Scientific Publishing Services, Chennai, India

Printed on acid-free paper

Springer is part of Springer Science+Business Media (www.springer.com)

Preface

Message from the General Chairs

CollabTech 2014, the 7th International Conference on Collaboration Technologies, offered a unique forum for academics and practitioners to present and discuss innovative ideas, methods, or implementations related to collaborations technologies, which are greatly needed for various everyday collaborations due to marked advances in networking, computing, and interaction technologies.

The previous CollabTech conferences were held in Tokyo in 2005, Tsukuba in 2006, Seoul in 2007, Wakayama in 2008, Sydney in 2009, and Sapporo in 2012. CollabTech 2014 was co-located and organized with CRIWG 2014 in Santiago, Chile. CRIWG and CollabTech communities had similar research topics and goals, but had been geographically located in different regions. We believed this joint endeavor would provide an interesting opportunity to meet each other across the Pacific Ocean in the genial spring weather of Santiago.

Another change to note was that the proceedings of this conference were published online in the CCIS series by Springer. We hope that this improved the availability and circulation of the presented research. The success of the conference was largely due to the program co-chairs, the conference committee members, and the reviewers whose efforts made the conference possible. The success was also due to the Department of Management and Control Systems and the Department of Computer Science of the University of Chile, the SIG on Groupware and Network Services of the Information Processing Society of Japan, the SIG on Cyberspace of the Virtual Reality Society of Japan, and the SIG on Communication Enhancement of the Human Interface Society for their generous support. Hitachi, Ltd. contributed financially to the success of the conference.

We are pleased that the conference was fruitful for all participants and played an important role in cultivating the community in this research field.

September 2014

Nelson Baloian
Tomoo Inoue
Hiroaki Ogata

Message from the Program Chairs

After six events in the International Conference on Collaboration Technologies series, we had the seventh edition (CollabTech 2014) in Santiago, Chile. The following topics on collaboration technologies were discussed:

- Collaborative Problem Solving
- Knowledge Work and CSCW Tasks
- Co-Dining Support
- Augmented Reality and Robots
- Learning Support Systems

For this conference, we received 34 submissions (24 full papers, 10 short papers) and assigned three reviewers per full paper or two reviewers per short paper. As a result, we had ten full papers and four short papers. The acceptance rate was 41%. The accepted papers represented eight countries from all over the world, reflecting the international recognition of CollabTech 2014.

Without our distinguished Program Committee members, we could not have maintained our high standards. We truly appreciated their devotion. Finally, we hoped that these proceedings serve as a reference for future researchers in this rapidly evolving field.

September 2014   Takaya Yuizono
                                                                 Gustavo Zurita

Organization

General Co-chairs

Nelson Baloian   Universidad de Chile, Chile
Tomoo Inoue   University of Tsukuba, Japan
Hiroaki Ogata   Kyushu University, Japan

Program Committee Co-chairs

Takaya Yuizono   Japan Advanced Institute of Science and Technology, Japan
Gustavo Zurita   Universidad de Chile, Chile

Financial Co-chairs

Nobutaka Kawaguchi   Hitachi, Ltd., Japan
Takefumi Ogawa   The University of Tokyo, Japan

Publicity Co-chairs

Takashi Yoshino   Wakayama University, Japan
Masaki Omata   Yamanashi University, Japan

Publication Co-chair

Junko Ichino   University of Kagawa, Japan
Hidekazu Shiozawa   Tamagawa University, Japan

IPSJ SIG GN Liaison

Satoshi Ichimura   Tokyo University of Technology, Japan

VRSJ SIG CS Liaison

Kazuyuki Iso   NTT, Japan

HIS SIG CE Liaison

Yutaka Ishii   Okayama Prefectural University, Japan

Steering Committee

Hideaki Kuzuoka	University of Tsukuba, Japan
Ken-ichi Okada	Keio University, Japan
Jun Munemori	Wakayama University, Japan
Minoru Kobayashi	NTT, Japan

Program Committee

Hui-Chun Chu	Soochow University, Taiwan
Hironori Egi	Kobe University, Japan
Kinya Fujita	Tokyo University of Agriculture and Technology, Japan
Atsuo Hazeyama	Tokyo Gakugei Unversity, Japan
Adam Hou	National Tsing Hua University, Taiwan
Gwo-Jen Hwang	National Taiwan University of Science and Technology, Taiwan
Satoshi Ichimura	Tokyo University of Technology, Japan
Yutaka Ishii	Okayama Prefectural University, Japan
Kazuyuki Iso	NTT, Japan
Marc Jansen	University of Applied Sciences Ruhr West, Germany
Jongwon Kim	Gwangju Institute of Science and Technology, Korea
Hyungseok Kim	Konkuk University, Korea
Jee-In Kim	Konkuk University, Korea
Wim Lamotte	Hasselt University, Belgium
Ee-Peng Lim	Singapore Management University, Singapore
Chen-Chung Liu	National Central University, Taiwan
Tun Lu	Fudan University, China
Wolfram Luther	University of Duisburg-Essen, Germany
Hideyuki Nakanishi	Osaka University, Japan
Mamoun Nawahdah	Birzeit University, Palestine
Masayuki Okamoto	Toshiba, Japan
Masaki Omata	University of Yamanashi, Japan
Nobuchika Sakata	Osaka Univerisity, Japan
Yoshiaki Seki	Tokyo City University, Japan
Hidekazu Shiozawa	Tamagawa University, Japan
Daniel Spikol	Malmö University, Sweden
Masahiro Takatsuka	The University of Sydney, Australia
Julita Vassileva	University of Saskatchewan, Canada
Hao-Chuan Wang	National Tsing Hua University, Taiwan
Takashi Yoshino	Wakayama University, Japan

Keynote Talk

How Analytics Tools Can Support Learning Communities

H. Ulrich Hoppe

Department of Computer Science and Applied Cognitive Science
Faculty of Engineering, University of Duisburg-Essen
Building LF, Lotharstr. 63/65
47048 Duisburg, Germany
hoppe@collide.info

Abstract. In the area of computer-supported collaborative learning (CSCL), the methodology of social network analysis (SNA) has been used to identify roles and internal structures in learning groups. SNA has become an important tool to provide information and insight for managing learning communities. It is still a challenge to combine SNA with other techniques focusing on the analysis of content in learner-created artefacts or on the analysis of time-dependent patterns in learner activities. Several examples of applying such analyses to learning environments and communities will be given. Also, a general web-based workbench for creating and performing analysis workflows of different types will be presented. From a systems engineering point of view, the question of how to integrate analytics modules with existing learning environments and community platforms will be addressed.

Table of Contents

Learning Support Systems

CollPhoto: A Paper + Smartphone Problem Solving Environment for Science and Engineering Lectures

Claudio Alvarez[1], Marcelo Milrad[2], Francisco Borie[1], and Martín Luna[1]

[1] Facultad de Ingenieria y Ciencias Aplicadas, Universidad de los Andes, Santiago, Chile
[2] Department of Media Technology, Linnaeus University, Växjö, Sweden
calvarez@uandes.cl,
marcelo.milrad@lnu.se,
{fjborie,mluna}@miuandes.cl

Abstract. Recent studies in science and engineering education support that inductive learning activities encouraging active student involvement may improve students' motivation, development of soft skills and academic performance, compared to traditional lectures. Until recently, several technology-enhanced learning environments have been proposed to facilitate such activities in classrooms. However, these commonly depend on dedicated hardware devices, such as clickers or tablet PCs. Contrastingly, smartphones are being massively adopted by society as these become increasingly powerful and inexpensive. Even so, the use of smartphones as learning tools in lecture halls has still not been widely adopted. In this paper we present CollPhoto, a paper-plus-smartphone environment that supports face-to-face problem solving activities in the classroom. CollPhoto provides the instructor with instant visibility of students' work, and facilitates him/her conducting discussions, based on a selection of students' responses. We report on the design and initial validation of CollPhoto in the context of two computer science courses.

Keywords: STEM education, face-to-face problem solving, paper-plus-smartphone environment.

1 Introduction

In traditional Science, Technology, Engineering and Mathematics (STEM) undergraduate education, student cohorts are generally numerous, meaning that tenths or even hundredths of students may attend a lecture hall. During the lecture, the instructor will remain unaware of students' understanding of the factual, conceptual and procedural knowledge that has been transmitted to them. On the other hand, the students will have little chance to apply knowledge to problems and obtain formative feedback from the instructor (Felder et al., 2011; Wieman, 2007).

Recent studies in the fields of STEM education and Technology-Enhanced Learning (TEL) support that the use of inductive teaching methods (Prince & Felder, 2006) may actively engage students in learning during lectures, and in this way enhance their motivation, performance and learning outcomes compared to traditional instruction

T. Yuizono et al. (Eds.): CollabTech 2014, CCIS 460, pp. 1–15, 2014.

approaches (Deslauriers et al., 2011). These are many activities including, but not limited to, peer discussion approaches supported by classroom response systems and classroom presenters (Crouch et al., 2007; Deslauriers et al., 2011), and technology-supported collaboration scripts (i.e. CSCL scripts) for individual and collaborative problem solving (Baloian & Zurita, 2009; Nussbaum et al., 2009; Looi et al., 2010). While these technology-supported activities may actively engage students in learning and provide them quick formative feedback from the instructor, they require training, expensive hardware and technical support, imposing a cost burden to the academic staff, schools and faculties.

Pen and paper have been ubiquitous resources in traditional STEM education. Students have used pen and paper for their own personal annotations during lectures and recitations, and for solving problems from textbooks and class material. Researchers have argued that paper is a universal resource that can be integrated with digital technologies, such as mobile phones, to support learning activities (Huang et al., 2012). Indeed, inexpensive smartphones nowadays feature easy Wi-Fi and cellular data connectivity, increasingly fast CPUs and high-resolution cameras. While smartphones are increasingly adopted by higher education students, and brought by them to the lectures, pedagogic use of these devices in lecture halls is still not common practice. This latest fact opens up compelling opportunities for exploring inductive learning approaches for STEM lectures supported by paper and smartphones.

In this paper we present CollPhoto, a paper plus smartphone problem-solving environment for STEM classrooms that aims to engage students in active problem solving, while providing the instructor awareness of students' work and means to conduct discussions based on students' responses to the problems. In the next sections, we present the rationale and motivation for our work, the design of CollPhoto's pedagogical flow, technical implementation details and our evaluation plan.

2   Motivation and Rationale

Although current STEM students and instructors are surrounded by an unprecedented variety of technological devices, and the current generation of higher education students falls into the category of Millennials (Felder et al., 2011), still to these days, in STEM lecture halls use of smartphones and laptops is often discouraged, as students often tend to multitask and distract in online social activities and gaming rather than paying attention to the lecture. Pedagogical innovations departing from traditional practice, and requiring complex technologies, will not be welcomed and adopted by institutions while these pose high cost and risk burden to be successfully implemented (Pundak & Rozner, 2008). Hence, the possibility of using smartphones as learning tools in the lectures has not been widely acknowledged nor endorsed by STEM departments and faculties.

For students in STEM disciplines, problem-solving activities are one major way through which they acquire the knowledge they learn and on which they are assessed. However, typical student cohorts are numerous, thus limited time can be dedicated by the instructor or the teaching assistant to support students in problem solving activities in and outside the classroom (Wieman, 2007). In a typical lecture, the instructors will remain unaware of the students' learning progress unless effective formative assessment and feedback technologies are implemented (Crouch et al., 2007).

Different systems reported in the literature have relied on the use of mobile devices with digital ink affordances (Baloian & Zurita, 2009), or digital pens (e-pens or *smartpens*) and regular paper (Alvarez et al., 2013; Miura et al., 2007), to support constructivist problem solving activities, providing the instructor with a quick view of students' work. In these activities, the instructor can see on his/her device's screen the solutions to a given problem in digital ink format, and have them also in paper when e-pens are used. In this way, the instructor can provide formative feedback to the students, and mediate discussions in small groups and also involving the entire class group. Some of these approaches incorporate automated procedural scaffolds for collaborative work (Nussbaum et al., 2009), while others require greater mediation and scaffolding from the instructor (Looi et al., 2010). In a present-day lecture hall, this kind of workflow may be implemented relying on readily available resources: students' smartphones featuring photo cameras, pen and paper, and a projector screen.

We propose CollPhoto as a learning environment for supporting problem solving activities in STEM lectures and recitations. Students solve problems using pen and paper, individually or in dyads, take snapshots of their solutions with their smartphones, and share them with the instructor. The instructor relies on a user interface tailored for receiving and revising a large number of responses, and selecting among these answers that he/she may use in favor of providing the students formative feedback, as well as engaging them in directed dialogue and exploratory talk. In the present paper we report on the implementation and early evaluation of CollPhoto. We address the following research questions: (RQ1) Is the learning flow proposed by CollPhoto suitable for supporting problem solving activities in lecture halls with numerous STEM student cohorts? (RQ2) How is the value of social interaction and information sharing, enable by CollPhoto, perceived by teachers and students? (RQ3) Can the classroom discussions supported by CollPhoto provide the students meaningful formative feedback?

3   CollPhoto' Learning Flow

CollPhoto activities are based on the CSCL script (Dillenbourg, 2002) depicted in Fig. 1 below. Before the class starts, the instructor defines the tasks that will be presented to the students. He/she may upload a PDF file with detailed problem statements for each task, which the students can later download to their smartphones once the classroom activity has started. The instructor may configure each task's group composition, specifying whether the task should be solved individually or in dyads. If one or more of the tasks are planned be solved in dyads, the instructor may choose to sit the students randomly in the classroom.

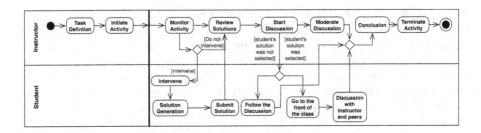

Fig. 1. The CollPhoto learning flow

In the lecture, the instructor starts each task by briefing the students on the problem statement and the objectives, specifying the time that is available for uploading solutions, and presenting the students a numeric identifier for the work session that is automatically generated by CollPhoto. The students log into CollPhoto in their own devices by using their university's email account credentials — they may choose to stay logged in, so that they omit this step in later sessions. They then enter the numeric identifier provided by the instructor, and start working individually or in dyads, solving the problem with pen and paper. The instructor monitors the activity, awaiting responses from the students in the classroom computer and/or in his/her mobile device (i.e. laptop, tablet or smartphone). The students submit a snapshot of each written page by means of CollPhoto's user interface in the mobile Web browser.

(a)   (b)

Fig. 2. (a) Instructor's visualization students' solutions. (b) Comparison of two solutions.

As the instructor receives responses from the students, he/she scans through them on his mobile device's interface seeking for different solution strategies, common misconceptions and errors, or any other noticeable characteristics in the responses worth of discussing and analyzing later with the students (Fig. 2a). He/she selects a subset of the answers he/she considers the most relevant regarding these aspects. When time is up, the instructor shows the selected answers on the projector screen. The CollPhoto interface displayed on the projector screen will allow the instructor to compare two responses at a time, side-by-side, taking up all the available space on the screen (Fig. 2b). The instructor may also choose to show a set of answers simultaneously in smaller size. He/she discusses the different solutions with the students, and he/she may call the authors of the solutions to the front of the class to explain their own approaches, strategies and reasoning.

Similarly to the Collpad and Collboard CSCL scripts (Nussbaum et al., 2009; Alvarez et al., 2013), in CollPhoto the teacher engages the whole class in a discussion after previous individual work and/or work in small groups concludes. The teacher-mediated classroom discussion in CollPhoto may involve directed dialogue with the students, exploratory talk and collective reflection on the different solutions.

4 Technological Implementation

4.1 Development Team

CollPhoto's development team has involved two undergraduate computer engineering students guided by the responsible researcher. The students have been in charge of most of the software development, and have assisted the responsible researcher in the in-class validation of the system. In addition, the development team invited three professors of mathematics, physics and electrical engineering subjects for co-design meetings at the beginning of the development process.

4.2 Development Process

Contrastingly to predictive research, which pursues solving complex problems by means of direct application of theories, we are developing CollPhoto following an iterative Design Based Research (DRB) process (Alvarez et al., 2011; Plomp, 2009). Our intent is to follow an iterative process of 'successive approximation' of the 'ideal' classroom interventions that are desirable with CollPhoto, through cycles of instructional design, software development, validation in real educational settings, and improvement and refinement of the tools and methods based on the obtained feedback. After defining the instructional design depicted in Fig. 1, we designed and implemented our first working prototype drawing on previous experiences developing Collpad (Nussbaum et al., 2009) and Collboard (Alvarez et al., 2013) systems. Our process began with definition of user and system requirements, covering both functional and non-functional specifications. Among the non-functional requirements that guided our design decisions, we established the following essential requirements:

- **Minimize Initialization and Setup Time.** Given time limitations for CollPhoto use during the lecture time, the application must be easily accessible by any mobile device at any time, with minimum interaction costs for the user.
- **Device Agnosticism.** The need to support different mobile devices provided by the students regardless of the operating system and form factor.
- **Sharing of Mobile Devices among Students.** The possibility of students being able to lend/borrow their mobile devices to/from each other to submit responses to the instructor should there not be enough mobile devices available in the classroom.
- **Large Number of Mobile Devices.** The need to support a large number of mobile devices (i.e. 40 to 100 devices) connected to a local WiFi network, allowing concurrent upload of high-resolution images to the server.

For the elicitation of functional requirements, we built low fidelity prototypes of the entire user interface using Balsamic Mockups software, a series of Unified Modeling Language (UML) activity diagrams depicting the workflow of classroom activities, and created domain and use case models of the system. Early validation of the user interface was conducted through two co-design meetings with three professors of mathematics, physics and electrical engineering subjects, lasting 1.5 hours each.

The implementation effort of the first CollPhoto prototype took eight weeks in total. The first three weeks focused on software analysis and design. The following five weeks were dedicated to development and laboratory testing of the system utilizing the abovementioned technologies, with three incremental deliveries of the software.

4.3   System Architecture

CollPhoto is based on the Ruby on Rails web application framework version 4, thus it is based on the well-known MVC architectural pattern tailored for web applications. In order to support different mobile devices and form factors (i.e., 'device agnosticism'), the entirety of the user interface is implemented in HTML 5, CSS3 and Javascript, relying mainly on the Twitter Bootstrap framework for responsive user interface design, and the jQuery framework for client-side programming. CollPhoto is hosted in an Amazon Web Services' Elastic Cloud Computing (EC2) virtual private server, and is served through the Thin HTTP server software in cluster mode behind an Nginx reverse proxy server (Coumoyer, 2014). The database system used is PostgreSQL, which operates in the same EC2 server that hosts the application. Fig. 3 depicts the basic connectivity configuration for CollPhoto and the software stacks used in client and server sides. One of the main reasons for deploying CollPhoto as a web application is the issue connected to easiness of access. Neither the students nor the teacher are required to install native applications on their devices, thus initialization and setup time for CollPhoto activities in the classroom is minimized.

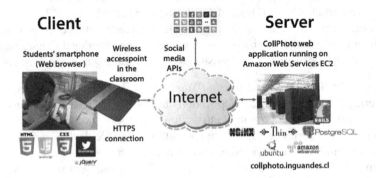

Fig. 3. CollPhoto client-server connectivity and software stacks

Our chosen architecture is flexible and expandable and we plan to integrate Coll-Photo with social media Application Programming Interfaces (APIs), such as the Evernote API (2014) and Disqus (2014), so that it can support storage and sharing of student-generated content in/from personal online notebooks, as well as discussing the shared content in discussion threads.

5   Early Validation of CollPhoto

We started the validation of CollPhoto in university classroom settings with the aim to conduct a formative evaluation (Bannan-Ritland, 2003; Alvarez et al., 2011) of the classroom workflow and supporting mobile tools. The formative evaluation comprised two successive trials. The first trial was conducted in March 2014 and focused on evaluating the technical and practical feasibility of conducting CollPhoto activities in classrooms. The trial was carried out on the Introduction to Computer Programming course (henceforth ICP course), held at Universidad de los Andes, Santiago, Chile. The course enrolled a total of 98 students divided into two groups, and Coll-Photo validation was conducted in the first group with 40 students. The second trial was conducted during April 2014 in the Relational DataBases course (henceforth RDB course) at U. de los Andes, with an enrolment of 87 students. During the second trial four instances of the CollPhoto learning flow were implemented, and after the trial the students were surveyed, and the teacher was interviewed. This trial was conducted aiming to respond research questions RQ1, RQ2 and RQ3 (see section 2).

5.1   Academic Context

The ICP and RDB courses in which CollPhoto underwent its first formative evaluation have been previously reformed to adopt a learning workflow based on the Just-in-Time Teaching (JiTT) blended learning approach (Novak et al., 1999; Prince & Felder, 2006). The RDB course was the first reformed during the spring semester (August-December) 2012, while the ICP course was reformed in the following semester (March-July 2013).

Under the JiTT methodology, students are responsible for studying the course contents by themselves (i.e., tutorials, videos and documentation) and answering online multiple-choice quizzes before attending the first weekly face-to-face lecture. The RDB course has a single weekly lecture lasting four successive modules of 50 minutes each, i.e. 200 minutes of total class time. On the other hand, the ICP course has two weekly face-to-face lectures, each lasting two successive modules of 50 minutes, i.e., 100 minutes of total class time in each lecture. Both courses are conducted in lecture halls equipped with WiFi network, and a projector screen attached to a computer intended for instructor's use. During the lectures, the instructor gives the students formative feedback on the previous online quiz and further explains and discusses contents in which the students revealed weaknesses. Then the students solve a series of problems of increasing difficulty using pen and paper individually or in dyads, under the teacher's and teaching assistants' supervision and guidance.

After time is up for solving a problem, the students' answer sheets are collected and the teacher explains the students about different possible ways of solving the problem before proceeding to the next one. In the traditional course workflow, although students' answers are collected before the teacher's feedback, the teacher does not rely on students' responses when commenting the solution to the problem due to his inability to revise the responses beforehand.

The instructor of the ICP course works part-time at the Engineering Faculty and has three years of teaching experience. The other instructor in charge of the RDB course is part of the fulltime academic staff at the Faculty. He has seven years of teaching experience.

5.2   Smartphone Ownership and Use Habits Survey

In order to establish whether students in the ICP and RDB courses could participate in the CollPhoto trials and use their own smartphones, we conducted an anonymous survey regarding smartphone ownership and use habits. All the students in both courses were encouraged by the respective instructors to answer the survey that included six binary and multiple-choice questions regarding smartphone ownership and use habits. The survey was conducted by means of the learning management system officially used in the courses, and was available to the students for an entire week.

The survey questions and answer options are described in Table 1.

Table 1. Smartphone Ownership and Use Habits Survey

#	Question	Answers
1	Do you own a smartphone?	(a) Yes, (b) I do not have a smartphone but a feature phone,, (c) I do not have a mobile phone
2	What kind of smartphone do you own?	(a) Android, (b) iOS (Apple iPhone), (c) Windows Phone, (d) Blackberry, (e) Other kind of smartphone
3	Do you connect to the Internet with your smartphone?	(a) No, (b) Yes (via WiFi or prepaid), (c) Yes (permanent connection)
4	Do you use instant messaging applications in your smartphone based on the Internet, such as WhatsApp, Telegram, etc?	Yes/No
5	Is the smartphone essential to you?	Yes/No
6	Would you feel upset if you do not have your smartphone for an entire day?	Yes/No

5.3   Trial in the ICP Course

A week before the first session of the trial, the responsible researcher met the ICP course instructor for a briefing and tutorial on CollPhoto. Problem design criteria was discussed, stressing the need to pose the students with open-ended problems that could elicit a variety of responses, so that the responses could later lead to a meaningful discussion based on different solution approaches.

The trial for feasibility evaluation was conducted in two lectures of the ICP course, in two successive weeks. Both lectures were the first in their respective weeks and the students' work was not graded; hence, evaluation of CollPhoto could be conducted minimizing the chance of a negative effect on the students' grades. The CollPhoto activities were conducted in the second 50-minute module of the ICP course lectures. The subject matter on which the problems were based was related to flow control in the Python programming language. The CollPhoto development team composed of the responsible researcher and two research assistants attended the two lectures and took notes of all technical issues encountered. In addition, after each of the two lectures the responsible researcher had a short interview with the course professor in order to collect his feedback on the activities conducted.

Before proceeding to the trial in the RDB course, the development team focused on solving all technical issues encountered.

5.4   Trial in the RDB Course

After major technical issues noticed in the initial technical feasibility evaluation could be overcome, the second trial for ascertaining teachers' and students' perceived pedagogical value and usability of CollPhoto was conducted in the RDB course. In the same manner as in the previous trial, the responsible researcher met beforehand with the professor in charge of the course for a quick briefing and training session.

The trial in the RDB course was conducted within a single lecture lasting four 50-minute modules. In the third module of the lecture, the instructor gave the students a briefing on the CollPhoto activity and displayed on the projector screen a list of instructions to connect to the WiFi network and to the CollPhoto website from their smartphones. After the students connected from their smartphones, four successive Structured Query Language (SQL) problems were posed to them. The entire CollPhoto workflow, including the teacher-guided discussion, was applied for all problems.

At the end of the lecture, the students were presented with an anonymous paper-based survey. The survey questions focused on capturing the students' perceived pedagogical value and ease-of-use (see Table 2) of CollPhoto.

In addition to the questions in Table 2, the students were also required to indicate their gender, age and year of entrance to engineering studies at U. de los Andes.

After the lecture was finished, the responsible researcher had a twenty-five minute unstructured interview with the professor of the RDB course. The views, observations and feedback from the instructor regarding usability and perceived pedagogical value of CollPhoto were transcribed by the responsible researcher during the interview.

Table 2. Students' survey regarding perceived pedagogical value and ease of use of CollPhoto

#	Question	Answers
1	Are you interested in the course's current subject matter?	Likert Scale (LS) (values 1–5)
2	Do you think the teacher's guided discussion involving the student's answers to the problem adds value to the lecture?	LS (values 1–5)
3	If the teacher calls you to the front to explain your answer to your peers, would you be willing to do it?	LS (values 1–5)
4	Do you feel the teacher was more accessible to addressing to your doubts and comments in the lecture than in the past ones?	LS (values 1–5)
5	Do you consider that submitting your solutions through CollPhoto in your smartphone is easy to use?	LS (values 1–5)
6	Please mention any aspects regarding Collboard that you would high-light	Open-ended
7	Please mention any aspects regarding Collboard that should be im-proved	Open-ended

6   Early Findings

6.1   Smartphone Ownership and Use Habits Survey

The smartphone ownership and use habits survey was responded by 49/98 (50%) students in the two sections of the ICP course, and by 65/87 (74,7%) students in the RDB course. In the first question, regarding smartphone ownership, 48/49 (97,9%) respondents in the ICP course and 60/65 (92,3%) respondents in the RDB course declare owning a smartphone. In both courses, smartphone ownership was reportedly split evenly among iOS (Apple iPhone) and Android devices. In the ICP course, 22/49 declared owning an Android device, and 26/49 declared owning an iPhone. In the RDB course, 27/65 students declared owning an Android device, 31/65 an iOS device, and 2/65 a Windows Phone device.

With regard to Internet connectivity, 10/49 (20,4%) students in the ICP course and 7/65 (10,8%) respondents in the RDB course connect to the Internet through WiFi or a prepaid card, and 39/49 (79,5%) students in the ICP and 55/65 (84,6%) students in the RDB course have a permanent connection to the Internet. All respondents owning a smartphone in both courses reported usage of non-SMS instant messaging services based on the Internet.

When asked if the smartphone is regarded as essential, 42/49 respondents in the ICP course and 45/65 students in the RDB course responded affirmatively. Lastly, roughly half of the respondents (25/49 in the ICP and 34/65 in the RDB course) reported that they would feel upset by not having their mobile phone for an entire day.

The survey results show that the majority of the students in the samples owned an internet-capable smartphone at the time of the trials, and many of the students reported being emotionally attached to their device, insofar they would feel upset if deprived from it. Consequently, students could participate in Collphoto activities supported by their own hardware.

6.2   Trial in the ICP Course

In the first session of this trial, 28 students attended the lecture and it was possible for the instructor to conduct a complete CollPhoto activity. While the students worked in pairs and later the discussion was conducted, the following technical and logistical issues were encountered:

- **Students' Registration Issue:** Eight students were omitted from registration in the CollPhoto database and were unable to log in at the start of the activity. The students' had enrolled in the course later in the semester and their information was not timely available to the CollPhoto system.
- **Discussion Interface Problems:** The CollPhoto interface supporting the teacher-guided discussion did not function properly when operated with a touchpad device in a laptop. It had been optimized for touchscreen devices, thus basic operations like dragging and scrolling did not work properly on the teacher's laptop computer connected to the projector screen.
- **Poor Time Management:** The students were not given a clear time limit to submit their responses, thus they worked relaxed, with no time pressures. The activity was conducted during the last 35 minutes of the second lecture module. After 25 minutes from the start of the activity only 6/14 dyads had submitted a response. The professor dedicated the remaining 10 minutes to conduct the discussion with the six available responses.

At the end of the trial, the instructor reported his own satisfaction with the discussion that was accomplished. Despite the limited number of submitted responses from the students, he could take advantage of recurrent mistakes he observed in the answers, and engage the students in a fruitful discussion.

In the second session of the trial, conducted in the following week, a major technical issue occurred, which hampered the completion of the CollPhoto activity:

- **Denial of Uploads:** CollPhoto used a naming convention for image files that appeared suspicious as a malware threat to the firewall software that filters Internet traffic in the entire university network. Consequently, the students were unable to submit their responses through CollPhoto and the activity was halted.

Fortunately, all of the technical issues encountered in the first trial could be solved with minimal effort. The students missing in the Collboard database were included for the second session of the trial, and the discussion interface could be made compatible with touchpad/trackpad interaction. The issue regarding the denial of image uploads to the server was solved by incorporating the use of secure HTTP connections (HTTPS). In this way, the university firewall is unable to filter the outgoing traffic from the students' devices to the server.

Despite the technical issues that occurred, the instructor of the ICP course mentioned that he would be willing to continue trying Collphoto in his lectures. He considered that CollPhoto's learning flow was practical for the course, and could support him in providing the students richer feedback. He also reported that the possibility of quickly visualizing the students' answers is useful for realizing what the common students' weaknesses and misconceptions are. He regarded this as valuable information that could lead him to improve the quality of his teaching.

6.3   Trial in the RDB Course

Classroom Activity Observation: Sixty-three students attended the trial lecture in the RDB course. At the beginning of the classroom activity a few students experienced difficulties connecting to the WiFi network, but managed to do so after few attempts. Once connected to the WiFi network from their smartphones, all of the students could log into the system.

The four SQL problems presented to the students covered database table creation, data insertion and query statements at beginner's level difficulty. Five minutes were given to the student dyads to solve each problem, and the successive teacher-guided discussion took a similar time span in each case. Under these time restrictions, task 3 had the most submitted responses (28), and task 4 the least (22). Despite that the CollPhoto learning flow includes the possibility of students being called to the front to explain their answers, the instructor did not encourage this to happen. Rather, he leaded the discussions and occasionally prompted the students for answers to his questions. Bidirectional and multidirectional dialogues between the instructor and the students were frequently noticed during the discussions, for clarification and reflection on the different solution approaches that were examined.

Interview with the Instructor: The instructor reported that the operation of the CollPhoto software during the trial lecture did not pose disruptive overhead to the classroom workflow that he had accustomed to conduct in the course for more than three semesters. Rather, he felt satisfied with the time efficiency of the workflow, as he managed to conduct all of the planned classroom activities in a timely manner.

According to the instructor, in all previous RDB course lectures, after the students finished each problem he had always relied on a single correct solution displayed on the projector screen to give the students formative feedback. With CollPhoto, in each of the four discussions in the trial lecture, he had made systematic use of the answer comparison tool to examine different students' responses. He considered that the tool was useful for giving the students richer feedback based on their own mistakes and misconceptions, and that he could have used it to a more beneficial extent in this regard should the problem difficulty had been higher. He noticed that while the students solved the problems some dyads had a tendency of being competitive against each other to submit the correct response earliest as possible. He related this behavior to the fact that through CollPhoto the students had their responses visible to the scrutiny of their peers for the first time in the course; this further motivated some of the students to submit correct solutions to achieve both learning and peer recognition.

Regarding the use of hardware, the instructor suggested that he would prefer to use a tablet device rather than the fixed PC available at the front of the classroom, to monitor the activity and scan through the students' responses. He considers that by use of a tablet device he could move freely in the classroom assisting the students/dyads and better focus his interventions on the weaker students.

(a)   (b)

Fig. 4. (a) Dyads solving a problem in the DB course. (b) The instructor discussing students' submitted answers displayed on the CollPhoto interface.

Students' Survey Results: The survey (as described in section 5.4) was responded by 63/87 students enrolled in the course. The mean student age was 22.3 years, 51 students were male and 12 were female. Students' self-reported interest regarding the subject matter being learned in the course was slightly above neutral (question 1, $M=3.63/5.00$; $SD=0.96$). The students considered that the teacher's guided discussion involving the student's answers to the problem adds value to the lecture (question 2, $M=4.03/5.00$; $SD=0.95$). However, according to the response to question 3, the students do not report sufficient self-motivation to step to the front of the classroom to explain and justify their answers ($M=2.62/5.00$; $SD=1.10$).

Regarding the students' perception on whether CollPhoto increased the teacher's openness to respond to their doubts and comments, their average response to question 4 was above neutral ($M=3.40/5.00$; $SD=0.98$), however, lacking detailed classroom observation data for an objective comparison with the previous course lectures it is not possible to state an emphatic difference in this regard.

The students reported a positive perception on the ease of use of the interface, according to the response to question 5 ($M=3.87/5.00$; $SD=1.14$). Concerning this aspect, the two last open-ended questions of the survey add details on how the user interface and user experience could be improved. In the final open-ended questions, the students highlighted as positive characteristics of CollPhoto the possibility to obtain quick formative feedback from the instructor based on comparison and discussion of their own responses (20 responses), the overall interactivity that was possible (8 responses), the instantaneity and rapidness of the workflow supported by CollPhoto (4 responses), and ease of use of the user interface (3 responses).

In the last question of the survey the students were asked to mention aspects of CollPhoto that should be improved. Here 9 respondents mentioned that the answer upload step was too slow, and 2 students reported that they experienced WiFi network connectivity problems. Three students mentioned that CollPhoto should automatically rotate photos taken in landscape orientation to portrait.

Despite the technical shortcomings reported by the students, the CollPhoto activities were found practical for supporting problem solving activities in the classroom, rich social interaction was observed in the teacher-guided discussions, and both the instructor and the students valued the formative feedback that was possible.

7 Conclusions and Future Work

The initial validation conducted in two computer science courses indicates that is feasible to implement the proposed Collphoto learning workflow, under the usual time limitations of lectures, and relying on students' using their own smartphones and basic equipment commonly found in classrooms.

According to the instructors' experiences, the learning flow in CollPhoto is useful for providing the students with rich formative feedback, including discussion and analysis of different solution views and approaches. Through visualizing students' responses, the instructors have meaningful awareness on students' understanding, which can be useful for improving interventions for the benefit of the more challenged students. On the other hand, students' solutions being subject to peer scrutiny can be motivating for higher achieving students seeking peer recognition and positive reinforcement. The students perceived the instructors' formative feedback as valuable for their learning.

In the future, we plan to improve CollPhoto by enhancing the performance of the solution upload process and incorporating image-filtering algorithms for better readability of the handwritten answers in the projector screen. We also plan to implement and evaluate the use of online portfolios and social content sharing to permit out-of-class interaction between the students and the instructor. In order to discern when, how and for whom CollPhoto can be most effective, we will conduct thorough evaluation of the learning flow in different STEM courses. Finally, to ascertain impact of CollPhoto activities in learning achievement, we consider conducting quasi-experimental studies during an entire academic year.

Acknowledgements. Reseach supported by Fondo de Ayuda a la Investigación (FAI) grant provided by Universidad de los Andes, Santiago, Chile, and by Education Grant award provided by Amazon Web Services.

References

1. Alvarez, C., Alarcon, R., Nussbaum, M.: Implementing collaborative learning activities in the classroom supported by one-to-one mobile computing: A design-based process. The Journal of Systems & Software 84(11), 1961–1976 (2011)
2. Alvarez, C., Salavati, S., Milrad, M., Nussbaum, M.: Collboard: Fostering New Media Literacies in the Classroom through Collaborative Problem Solving Supported by Digital Pens and Interactive Whiteboards. Computers & Education 63, 368–379 (2013)

3. Baloian, N., Zurita, G.: MC-Supporter: Flexible Mobile Computing Supporting Learning though Social Interactions. Journal of Universal Computer Science 15(9), 1833–1851 (2009)
4. Bannan-Ritland, B.: The role of design in research: the integrative learning design framework. Educational Researcher 32(1), 21–24 (2003)
5. Coumoyer, M.-A.: Thin: A fast and very simple Ruby web server (2014), http://code.macournoyer.com/thin/usage (accessed April 17, 2014)
6. Crouch, C.H., Watkins, J., Fagen, A.P., Mazur, E.: Peer instruction: Engaging students one-on-one, all at once. Research-Based Reform of University Physics 1(1), 40–95 (2007)
7. Deslauriers, L., Schelew, E., Wieman, C.: Improved learning in a large-enrollment physics class. Science 332, 862–864 (2011), doi:10.1126/science.1201783
8. Disqus (2014), http://disqus.com/ (accessed April 20, 2014)
9. Evernote API (2014), http://dev.evernote.com/doc/ (accessed April 20, 2014)
10. Dillenbourg, P.: Over-scripting CSCL: the risks of blending collaborative learning with instructional design. In: Kirschner, P.A. (ed.), pp. 61–91. Open Universiteit Nederland, Heerlen (2002)
11. Felder, R.M., Brent, R., Prince, M.J.: Engineering instructional development: Programs, best practices, and recommendations. Journal of Engineering Education 100(1), 89–122 (2011)
12. Huang, H.-W., Wu, C.-W., Chen, N.-S.: The effectiveness of using procedural scaffoldings in a paper-plus-smartphone collaborative learning context. Computers & Education 59(2), 250–259 (2012), doi:10.1016/j.compedu.2012.01.015
13. Looi, C.-K., Chen, W., Ng, F.-K.: Collaborative activities enabled by GroupScribbles (GS): An exploratory study of learning effectiveness. Computers & Education 54(1), 14–26 (2010), doi:10.1016/j.compedu.2009.07.003
14. Miura, M., Kunifuji, S., Sakamoto, Y.: Practical environment for realizing augmented classroom with wireless digital pens. In: Apolloni, B., Howlett, R.J., Jain, L. (eds.) KES 2007, Part III. LNCS (LNAI), vol. 4694, pp. 777–785. Springer, Heidelberg (2007)
15. Novak, G.M., Gavrin, A., Wolfgang, C.: Just-in-time teaching: Blending active learning with web technology. Prentice Hall PTR (1999)
16. Nussbaum, M., Alvarez, C., Mcfarlane, A., Gomez, F., Claro, S., Radovic, D.: Technology as small group face-to-face Collaborative Scaffolding. Computers & Education 52(1), 147–153 (2009), doi:10.1016/j.compedu.2008.07.005
17. Plomp, T.: Educational design research: An introduction. In: An Introduction to Educational Design Research, pp. 9–35 (2009)
18. Prince, M.J., Felder, R.M.: Inductive Teaching and Learning Methods: Definitions, Comparisons, and Research Bases. Journal of Engineering Education, 123–138 (2006)
19. Pundak, D., Rozner, S.: Empowering Engineering College Staff to Adopt Active Learning Methods. Journal of Science Education and Technology 17(2), 152–163 (2008), doi:10.1007/s10956-007-9057-3
20. Wieman, C.: Why not try a scientific approach to science education? Change: The Magazine of Higher Learning 39(5), 9–15 (2007)
21. Zurita, G., Nussbaum, M.: Computer supported collaborative learning using wirelessly interconnected handheld computers. Computers and Education 42(3), 289–314 (2004)

The Use of a Maverick in Collaborative Problem Solving: Investigating the Implicit and Explicit Process

Yugo Hayashi[1] and Kazuaki Kojima[2]

[1] Department of Psychology, Ritsumeikan University
Toji-in Kitamachi, Kita-ku, Kyoto, Japan
[2] Learning Technology Laboratory, Teikyo University
1-1 Toukyoudai, Utsunomiya, Tochigi, Japan
y-hayashi@acm.org

Abstract. The present study focused on the implicit and explicit search processes for easing an impasse during collaborative problem solving. In this study, an attractive actor or an anomaly cue, a 'maverick,' appeared to aid the participant in a rule discovery task. Problem solvers works on the task in which autonomous agents play the roles of collaborative partners. We collected verbal responses and eye movement data throughout the task to capture the implicit and explicit cognitive processes used by participants in interacting with the maverick during the search activities. The results indicate that for successful problem solvers, (1) an anomaly cue(maverick) in the group explicitly facilitated an adequate search process, and (2) an implicit search process may exist from an early stage and may develop during the learning process through incubation. Additionally, we observed through case studies that participants actively use the anomaly cue(maverick) as a reference to ease impasses.

Keywords: Collaborative Problem Solving, Conversational Agents, Eye tracking, Verbalization.

1 Introduction

Imagine a software programmer who is confronted with a compile error, and no matter how hard he tries to fix the problem and no matter how much he thinks about it, he cannot find the solution he needs. Just when he starts to give up, he hears the programmer next to him murmuring while coding, and these words spark an idea. The next moment, the programmer is saying, 'Aha! I was just missing a semicolon at the end of my statement.'

In such a situation, the programmer is at an 'impasse,' and is searching for the solution in the wrong problem space[16,1,19]. Researchers studying insight have explained that it is important to relieve mental constraints and shift toward an adequate problem space to reach a solution[7]. Studies show that such constraints can be diminished by the use of external resources and environments that can

T. Yuizono et al. (Eds.): CollabTech 2014, CCIS 460, pp. 16–28, 2014.

provide meaningful cues[22]. In the example above, the neighboring programmer functioned as an external resource offering a cue.

The present study focuses on external resources such as human partners. Based on the past studies of [5], we focused in particular on a group structure in which a member called a 'maverick,' either an attractive actor or an anomaly cue, helps problem solvers search for an adequate problem space. The present study investigates the search processes specific to collaborative activities that can prevent impasses. We especially focused on the implicit and explicit cognitive processes that are mentioned in several prominent insight problem solving studies.

1.1 External Resources That Can Facilitate the Search Process: Collaborative Partners

Distributed cognition theories have brought us new views concerning the problem space where cognition could be extended to the external world[24,6]. Many studies in the area of collaborative problem solving in cognitive science have shown that internal representations can be changed by external resources such as collaborative partners[11,17]. Partners can play an important role in facilitating the meta cognitive process, which can help avoid cognitive biases. This occurs because feedback from others about the generated interpretations provides an opportunity to rethink the interpretation in a more reflective way[18]. Further, interacting with members leads to considering different perspectives[4],which can facilitate conceptual changes and deeper understanding[11]. In situations where one is at an impasse, member diversity(external world) can provide effective cues or hints to enable problem solvers to expand the areas of their problem solving space and reach the correct solutions.

What types of group formations, organizations, or compositions can become ideal cues for expanding the search space? An experiment conducted by [5] showed that a group consisting of members with different perspectives (i.e., the so-called 'maverick') can be effective when considering group differences; thus, these can act as anomaly cues that expand the search process. Evidence from organizational studies indicates that a person who holds a different perspective from the rest of the group may be perceived as a troublemaker that promotes confusion within the group. Sometimes, however, the person who sees things differently might be considered a reformer who brings innovative ideas to the group[14]. In the classic studies on 'minority effects' in social psychology, [12] argued that a minority of one is more influential than a minority of more than one. A series of studies have shown that if one person maintains the minority view, this idea may, over time, capture more attention[15]. Following these studies, the present research considered the effects of a maverick that eventually provided a hint to ease the impasse.

1.2 Two Types of Cognitive Processes: Implicit and Explicit

A maverick member(maverick) may provide crucial cues for searching the adequate problem space. What kinds of processes underlie the easing impasses given feedback from the maverick? Recent studies into insight problem solving show that two different processes, implicit and explicit, may be crucial factors in easing impasses.

Previous studies showed that people sometimes find a crucial cue relatively early in the problem solving process, but they cannot make use of it[22,7,10]. This indicates that some kind of implicit process may exist from the beginning of the task, and this may play an important role in the search for an adequate problem space.

How can we capture this implicit process during problem solving activities? A study conducted by [23], used eye-tracking data and verbalized data to capture both implicit and explicit cognitive processes during a rule discovery task. They showed that an implicit process captured from the eye-tracking data appeared gradually by focusing on a critical point related to the solution from an early problem solving stage. However, participants had no explicit knowledge of this process. The explicit process was captured from verbal protocol data from participants who suddenly reached the solution at some point. They admitted that an implicit process underlying the activity may have functioned to ease the impasse.

Our focus in this study was to investigate whether such an implicit process may exist while still interacting with an external resource(maverick) that may become a cue to easing an impasse. Our first goal in this study was as follows:

1. To investigate the role of implicit and explicit search processes in easing impasses in collaborative problem solving
2. To investigate how people use external resources(mavericks) to ease impasses

Based on past research, we hypothesized that an implicit searching process may begin before the explicit process. Moreover, external resources(mavericks) should be considered often by those who use them as effective cues. In investigating these points, this study not only uncovered implications about the implicit/explicit search mechanisms of how people ease from an impasse while collaborating with others, but it may also give some useful ideas to AI and HCI researchers in designing and developing effective intelligent collaboration-support systems.

2 Method

A controlled experiment was designed based on [5]'s, MAES, where a problem-solver engages in a rule discovery task with autonomous agents acting as collaborative partners. As many studies in the Media Equation literature have shown, there is much evidence that people respond to artificial agents [13]. Some studies have begun to use them as experimental tools for investigating human cognition [21], as in the present study.

2.1   The Rule Discovery Task: Bistable Objects

Participants were asked to count a series of objects presented on a computer display and to discover its sequential rule by cooperating with other collaborating members(conversational agents). Several sets of random patterns containing various figures on a 6 × 6 grid (colored black or white; see Figure 1) were shown to each participant. In each set, a pattern consisting of combined square blocks was displayed against a background of either black or white colors. The background color was controlled to derive, through a Gestalt effect, the change in the problem solver's perspective [8].

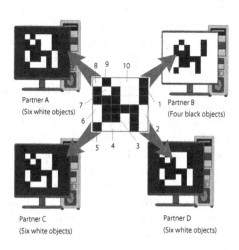

Fig. 1. Experimental stimuli used in the study

Each set consisted of several "objects" (or patterns) in black or white, each of which consisted of either a single block or multiple blocks. As shown in Figure 1, one of the paired objects contained a total of 10 objects (4 black and 6 white). When a participant focused on white components inside a black background, it was expected that the white objects would pop out as a figure and that the participants would be able to count all six of them.

In the present study, a group of six members were set to work collaboratively on the rule discovery task through a computer terminal connected via a local area network. Their goal was to count the number of objects presented on their screen for several trials and to discover the pattern rule for the number of presented objects. For each trial/set of objects, a square outer box was presented on the display for one second; this was followed by a stimulus picture inside the box frame. Participants were instructed to count the number of objects inside this box frame. They were also instructed that a software program called 'Agents' would be their partner, and that they would have to work together through textual feedbacks. The participant was required to verbalize any kind of relevant message(pertaining to number of objects, rules, etc.) per trial to the other collaborating members(agents).

As shown in Figure 1, participants saw the objects with either a black background (white perspective) or a white background (black perspective). To create a situation where a maverick existed in the task, the background color was adjusted for one of the members(agents). The majority of members saw the white object as the figure, and one(the maverick) saw a black object.

To create a situation where the problem solver is fixed in an impasse, the number of black and white objects were controlled, as shown in Figure 2. First, the total number of components presented to the participants varied between 6 and 10. The sequential pattern (Target rule) of the sums of black components and white components was repeatedly presented during each trial (e.g., 6,8,10,6,8,10...). In the initial (impasse forming) stage of the task, the local black/white numbers were controlled to be the same. Past studies showed that when problem solvers engaged in such a task, they only counted the objects based on the figure perspective, and participants tried to search for the target rule based on that perspective [4,3,5]. That is, they form an impasse of searching for the problem space, based on 'either' white or black objects, e.g. 3,4,5,3,4,5... After trial 13, the number of objects was controlled, so that one could not discover the rule based on the local colors(3,4,5,3,4,5...). The problem solvers could discover the rule only if they shifted their perspective toward 'both' black and white objects (6,8,10,6,8,10...). To discover the correct solution, they had to escape from the impasse(either color) in the initial stage and shift their perspective to the adequate problem solving space(both colors). Further, the maverick reported the number of objects based on the opposite-colored object, so this information served as a hint.

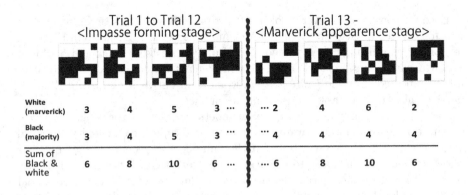

Fig. 2. Example object sequence

2.2   Experimental System

We set up a text-based chat communication platform by using one server and five conversational agents(Figure 3). The system was similar to one designed by [5] and developed in Java. On the server side, a broadcast mechanism was used to distribute all the messages simultaneously. On each trial, all agents responded to the problem solvers' utterances. The experimenter typed text messages of the participants verbal utterances and sent them to the server via chat. Messages sent to the server were redistributed to all agents.

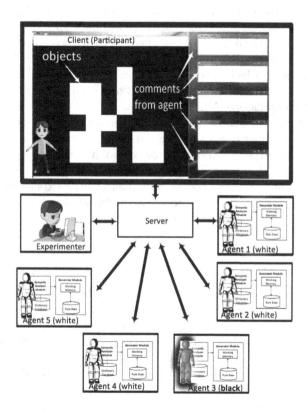

Fig. 3. Communication platform

The conversational computer agents were designed by a typical rule-based system. Based on predefined rules, the system could respond to sentences inputted by the participants (Figure 3). All three agents followed these rules: (1) respond only concerning the number and hypothesis in the impasse phase; (2) after the 13th trial, the maverick will sometimes include information about a different object (black); (3) do not respond in the same order for each trial; and (4) respond based on the input messages with which the last agent responded. All agents autonomously responded to each other's text messages as independent interlocutors using different types of expressions. However, Agent 3 was implemented to play the role of the maverick and thus responded based on the black-colored object.

The conversation agent extracted keywords from both the participant's and the other agents' sentences. The most frequent keywords related to the (1) number of objects, (2) colors of objects, and (3) sequence rules. The agent contained temporary working memory storage to represent the current status of the input messages from the: (1) keywords of the participant, (2) keywords from the agents, and (3) objects that were presented on the screen. A rule based in an "if-then" format defined all responses from the agents. When the agent detected keywords of: (a) numbers, (b) colors, and (c) the hypothesis, the working memory was updated. Then, a pattern-matching strategy was used for binding the rules. For example, outputs of numbers (black) and colors (black) could be, "Participant: I think there are four black objects...", "Agent 3: So you see four? I see six of them in black." "Agent 5: Black? I see four...," etc. The server would then distribute the messages to each agent in a randomized order with a delay for appropriate turn taking(for details, see [5]).

Each participant viewed an individual computer display with a resolution of 1920 x 1080. The upper edge of Figure 3 shows the interface of the display. The object was presented in the middle of the screen, and the agents' text responses were shown next to the figure. The participants were required to speak first, then read the comments from the agents, and then tell the experimenter to switch to the next slide(trial). The task continued until 30 minutes had passed; they could finish the task at that point when they mentioned the target rule to the experimenter.

2.3   Data Collection

We used two types of data to detect the implicit and explicit processes during the problem-solving space-search activities. We used the same indexes as [23]. First, the verbal utterances collected from the problem solvers' protocols were defined as the search process of the explicit state. Verbal data are mostly used by cognitive psychologists to detect problem solvers' internal states [2]. We calculated the ratio of the figure(black) and ground(white) in each trial and determined which problem space(color) the participants were fixated on. Then, each participant's verbal data were coded to either figure(white) or ground(black).

Second, we used eye movement data to record the participants' implicit search processes and their verbalizations concerning the detection of the explicit process. Insight problem solving studies use eye movement data as a useful index[9]. We used the Tobii eye tracking device(X2-30) to track participants' gaze behavior during the task. The sample rate was 30Hz. For analysis, we adapted the same procedure used with the verbal data. All retention data were collected for each trial and coded either to figure(white) or ground(black).

We used the modified version of the index from [4] to analyze the strength tendency of the impasse. In table 1, n_1 indicates the amount of reporting/looking at the figure(white), and n_2 indicates the amount of reporting/looking at the ground(black).

Table 1. Coding Scheme

	Figure (white)	Ground (black)
Participant	n_1	n_2

$$Impasse = \frac{n_1 - n_2}{n_1 + n_2} \tag{1}$$

The index indicates that the participant is most fixated on the figure color, and thus trapped in an impasse if the number is large. However, if the number gets smaller, this means that the participant is looking at the ground color and is searching for a different problem space. This leads to an easing of the impasse.

In addition, we analyzed the collected eye movement data on the text box in order to investigate how problem solvers use external resources to escape from the impasse.

3 Results

Twenty-one students(15 male, 6 female, average age $=$ 19.71), mostly information science, life science, and medical science majors from the University of Tsukuba participated in this experiment. We divided the participants who were successful in reporting answers related to the numbers of figure(white) color or ground(black) objects. Twelve succeeded, and nine did not.

4   Search Process on the Problem Space

Figure 4 shows the results of the experiment. The vertical axis represents the mean value of impasse for the measures listed on the horizontal axis. The horizontal axis shows each impasse phase(until the 12th trial) and maverick phase(after the 13th trial).The left figure shows the successful group, while the right shows the unsuccessful one.

A 2 × 2 ANOVA was conducted on each successful/unsuccessful group with the search methods (eye movements vs. verbal utterances) and the time(until the 12th trial vs. after the 13th trial) as mixed-subject factors. The results revealed an interaction between the two successful group factors $(F(1,22)=11.51, p <.01)$. Simple main effects for each search method by time revealed that eye movement values were higher than verbal utterance values until the 12th trial $(F(1,44)=28.57, p <.01)$, but there were no differences after the 13th trial $(F(1,44)=0.52, p=.48)$. In addition, simple main effects for each time by condition revealed that verbal utterance values decreased by time $(F(1,22)=18.77, p <.01)$, though there were no differences for the eye movements $(F(1,22)=0.22, p=.64)$.

There was no interaction between the two factors for the unsuccessful groups $(F(1,16)=0.97, p=.34)$. Main effects showed that the verbal utterances were higher than the eye movements $(F(1,16)=41.141, p <.01)$, but there were no differences between the time periods $(F(1,16)=0.32, p <.58)$. For the successful group, when the anomaly cue(maverick) appeared, the degree of impasse captured from verbal utterances reached the same level as that captured from the eye movements. Furthermore, the eye movements were steady at the same level throughout the task, indicating that an adequate early-stage search process had occurred. In contrast, for the unsuccessful pairs, the degree of impasse captured from verbal utterances was unchanged, indicating that anomaly cues(maverick) did not reach the implicit level.

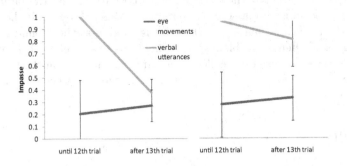

Fig. 4. Results of the successful(left) and unsuccessful(right)

5   Case Study: External Resources(Agents/Partners)

First, we analyzed the relative differences between the frequency of retention on each agent(partner). A one-way ANOVA was conducted on successful groups with the agents methods (agent1 vs. agent2 vs. agent3(maverick) vs. agent4 vs.agent5). For the successful group, there were differences among conditions $(F(11,44)=6.27, p <.01)$. The results of multiple comparisons showed that agent1 had a smaller glance tendency compared to agents 3,4, and 5 $(p <.01, p <.01, p <.01)$. However, there were no differences for the other conditions. These results reveal that agent3 was not especially attended as compared with the other agents. However, this may be attributable to the following: (1) some successful pairs did not use the external resource for the entire time; (2) since the majority of the agents continued to provide the same information, participants may have used a strategy of only looking at two important members, such as agent3(maverick) and some other agent close to it(e.g., agent 2 or agent 4). However, there might have been some data noise due to the differences among individuals and the diversity of the eye tracking data. Therefore, we conducted a more careful case study of the participants with the highest eye movement acquisition.

Figure 5 and figure 6 shows the transitions of two types of participants. The eye dots were expressed in the RGB format by time consumption(beginning of task to the end) by blue, purple, green, yellow, pink, and red. For the participant in figure 5, a total of 46397 points were collected; these were divided into three phases (First third, Second third, Third third). For the participant in figure 6,

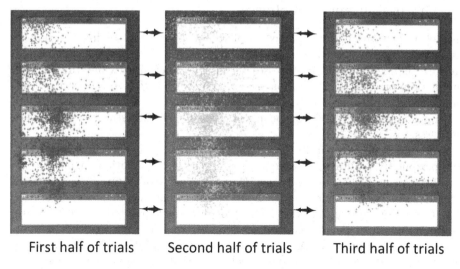

First half of trials   Second half of trials   Third half of trials

Fig. 5. Participant 1

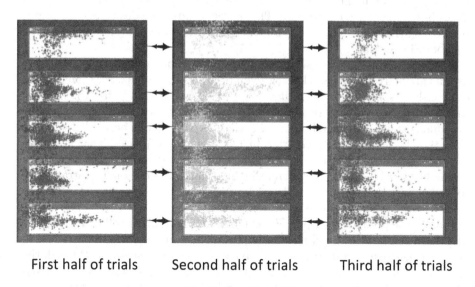

First half of trials   Second half of trials   Third half of trials

Fig. 6. Participant 2

a total of 43708 points were collected and also divided into three phases. As can be seen in figure 5, in the first half of the trial, the participant glanced more at agent 3(maverick). As time passed, this participant still looked at agent 3 more often. This indicates that the external resource could have had a special meaning to them on discovery. In contrast, in figure 6, the participant glances were based on agents 2 and 3. The participant might have been using a strategy to collect useful information from only the external sources.

6   Discussion and Conclusion

In the present study, we conducted a collaborative problem solving experiment using [5]'s MAES. We collected verbal utterances and eye movement data to capture implicit and explicit processes during search activities while studying the interactions of a maverick. The goal of this study was (1) to investigate the role of implicit and explicit search processes in easing impasses in collaborative problem solving, and (2) to examine how people use external resources(mavericks) to ease impasses.

The results showed that, for successful pairs, an anomaly cue(maverick) in the group explicitly facilitated an adequate search process. In addition, we found that an adequate implicit process was ongoing before such explicit processes occurred. This suggests a possible implicit incubation phase that may help explicit search due to the anomaly cue(maverick). This process could be related to the literature by [22,7,10], which found that people recognize crucial cues, but they cannot make proper use of them. As indicated from recent studies from [22], several types of constraints, such as object level, relational, and goal constraints exist and appear to be the causes for these impasses when they are gradually revealed by failures. A notable point here is that feedback from the external world plays a role in relaxing such constraints. The present study provides new implications by showing that such feedback can be demonstrated by a maverick opinion in a collaborative setting.

From the additional case study, we found that some problem solvers actively use the anomaly cue(maverick) as a reference to ease the impasse, though some do not show special interest in it at all. An interesting study from [20] shows that problem solvers who scan paths become well-organized problem solvers by becoming expert searchers. It is possible that, as participants proceeded with the task, they became more expert in seeing each agent's responses. That is, agents 1,2 and 4,5 always responded on the white perspective, while agent 3 reported on the black perspective. Therefore, the most efficient and economic strategy to collect important information from the others was to simply pay attention to agent3 or either one of the other four agents.

Finally, the present study provides evidence to suggest that collaborative partners, such as mavericks, can play an important role in easing an impasse and in directing us to an adequate problem solving space. This may occur through the existence of an implicit process due to such feedback from the external world and an effective use of the environment. Researchers in AI and computer-supported cooperative work (CSCW) can use the implications of this study to design collaborative systems in anticipation of increased creative performance. One important point here is that we used an artificial conversational agent; therefore, such agents can be used for easing impasses in problem solving settings.

Acknowledgements. This work was supported (in part) by 2012 KDDI Foundation Research Grant Program. The Grant-in-Aid for Scientific Research (KAKENHI), The Ministry of Education, Culture, Sports, Science, and Technology, Japan (MEXTGrant), Grant No. 25870910.

References

1. Dominowski, R.L., Dallob, P.: Insight and problem solving. In: Sternberg, R.J., Davidson, J.E. (eds.), pp. 33–62. MIT Press, Cambridge (1992)
2. Ericsson, K.A., Simon, H.A.: Protocol analysis: Verbal reports as data. MIT Press, Cambridge (1993)
3. Hayashi, Y., Miwa, K., Morita, J.: A laboratory study on distributed problem solving by taking different perspectives. In: Proceedings of the 28th Annual Conference of the Cognitive Science Society, pp. 333–338 (2006)
4. Hayashi, Y., Miwa, K.: Prior experience and communication media in establishing common ground during collaboration. In: Proceedings of the 31st Annual Conference of the Cognitive Science Society, pp. 526–531 (2009)
5. Hayashi, Y.: The effect of "maverick": a study of group dynamics on breakthrough in collaborative problem solving. In: Proceedings of the 34th Annual Conference of the Cognitive Science Society, pp. 444–449 (2012)
6. Hollan, J., Hutchins, E., Kirish, D.: Distributed cognition: Toward a new foundation for human-computer interaction research. ACM Transactions on Computer-Human Interaction 7(2), 174–196 (2000)
7. Kaplan, C.A., Simon, H.A.: In search of insight. Cognitive Psychology 22(3), 374–419 (1990)
8. Koffka, K.: Principles of gestalt psychology. Routledge and Kegan Paul (1935)
9. Knoblich, G., Ohlsson, S., Raney, G.E.: An eye movement study of insight problem solving. Memory and Cognition 27(7), 1000–1009 (2001)
10. MacGregor, J.N., Ormerod, T.C., Chronicle, E.P.: Information processing and insight: A process model of performance on the nine-dot and related problems. Journal of Experimental Psychology: Learning, Memory, and Cognition 27(1), 176–201 (2001)
11. Miyake, N.: Constructive interaction and the interactive process of understanding. Cognitive Science 10(2), 151–177 (1986)
12. Moscovici, S., Lage, E., Naffrechoux, M.: Influence of a consistent minority on the responses of a majority in a color perception task. Sociometry 32(4), 365–380 (1969)
13. Nass, C., Moon, Y., Fogg, B.J., Reeves, B., Dryer, D.C.: Can computer personalities be human personalities? International Journal of Human Computer Studies 43(2), 223–239 (1995)
14. Near, J.P., Miceli, M.P.: Whistle-blowers in organizations: Dissidents or reformers? Reserch in Organizational Behavior 9(4), 321–368 (1987)
15. Nemeth, C., Brown, K., Rogers, J.: Devil's advocate versus authentic dissent: stimulating quatity and quality. European Journal of Social Psychology 31(6), 707–720 (2001)
16. Ohlsson, S.: Information-processing explanations of insight and related phenomena. In: Keane, M., Gilhooley, K. (eds.), pp. 1–44. Harvester Wheatsheaf, London (1992)
17. Salomon, G.: Distributed cognition: Psychological and educational considerations. Cambridge University Press, New York (2001)
18. Shirouzu, H., Miyake, N., Masukawa, H.: Cognitively active externalization for situated reflection. Cognitive Science 26(4), 469–501 (2002)
19. Smith, S.M.: Getting into and out of mental ruts: A theory of fixation, incubation and insight. In: Sternberg, R.J., Davidson, J.E. (eds.), pp. 229–251. MIT Press, Cambridge (1992)

20. Stark, L., Ellis, S.R.: Scanpaths revisited: Cognitive models direct active looking. In: Fisher, D.F., Monty, R.A., Senders, J.W. (eds.), pp. 193–226. Lawrence Erlbaum Associates, NJ (1981)
21. Staudte, M., Crocke, M.: Investigating joint attention mechanisms through spoken human-robot interaction. Cognition 120(2), 268–291 (2011)
22. Suzuki, H., Abe, K., Hiraki, K., Miyazaki, M.: Cue-readiness in insight problem-solving. In: Proceedings of the 23rd Annual Meeting of the Cognitive Science Society, pp. 1012–1017 (2001)
23. Terai, H., Miwa, K.: Insight problem solving from the viewpoint of constraint relaxation using eye movement analysis. In: Proceedings of the 4th International Conference of Cognitive Science, pp. 671–676 (2003)
24. Zhang, J., Norman, D.A.: Representations in distributed cognitive tasks. Cognitive Science 18(1), 87–122 (1994)

Topic-by-Topic Activity Estimation
for Knowledge Work Lifelog

Masayuki Okamoto

Corporate R&D Center, Toshiba Corporation, Japan
masayuki4.okamoto@toshiba.co.jp

Abstract. We propose a topic-based activity review application that supports knowledge workers in reviewing activity history. This application automatically generates a knowledge work lifelog with event detection from sensor information, operation history, and used documents on a terminal; annotation term extraction considering topic estimation and collocation extraction; topic title extraction; and topic-based activity time calculation. This application enables activity review with a timeline view and activity overview with a calendar/graph view. According to an empirical evaluation with five subjects, we confirmed that the term extraction method is efficient for lifelog annotation and topic title extraction. We also identified challenges concerning determination of detailed activity time.

Keywords: Knowledge work, lifelog, topic model, LDA, C-value.

1 Introduction

The purpose of this paper is to propose a topic-based activity review application that supports knowledge workers in reviewing activity history with a summarized view of their activities by topic. Knowledge workers often review their own activity histories to write their daily or weekly reports, search some specific materials such as emails, schedules, and documents, or approximately calculate how much time they used for each task. However, it is difficult to review the activities as an aggregated history since these materials are scattered. To place the activities on time series data, gathering each user's activities on their terminal as a lifelog is a promising approach. However, it is difficult to review the sensor or operation events because users should interpret what they actually did from 'raw' large-scale lifelogs. We believe that users would like to review their lifelogs if this problem were solved.

One solution is to annotate activities after shrinking them into adequate volumes. Each annotation works as a summary of an activity and a search query so that users can interpret or search their activities easily. To realize this solution, a lifelogging application for knowledge workers, which considers topics and readability, has been proposed [8]. This application exploits text data for annotation, e.g., titles of emails, file names or content of documents. Although this system has a user interface for supporting activity review, it has been insufficient for overviewing activities for a wider time span, i.e., weekly or monthly review.

T. Yuizono et al. (Eds.): CollabTech 2014, CCIS 460, pp. 29–39, 2014.

In this paper, we introduced two overview modes: calendar view and graph view. Since lifelog events are classified for topics with topic models, users can review how much time they spent for each task. To realize these views, we introduce a topic-based activity estimation method based on topic modeling techniques. Our application includes lifelogging, annotation term extraction, topic title extraction, and activity time estimation by topic.

2   Related Works

Several researchers have endeavored to support review of knowledge work activities. The two principal approaches are search support and task classification.

The *search support* approach aims to help knowledge workers increase their efficiency by reducing the time and effort required to access relevant content or activities. FALCON is a system that integrates email and calendar functions with a recorded meetings application [1]. Using each person's microphone input, a method of searching documents used in a meeting without mail or calendar information is proposed [7].

The *task classification* approach aims to gather related applications or contents for each task so that a user can find the material needed for a selected task. An application to classify materials or documents from office work history, namely, TaskPredictor2, is proposed [10]. Activity Switch Detector focuses on activity switching [6].

Annotating terms extracted from documents corresponding to each lifelog event is a promising approach [8]. However, the timeline-based activity review UI is insufficient to overview activities weekly or monthly. We need an adequate activity time estimation method for reviewing knowledge work activity. In regard to requirements for these annotations, the ability to classify an activity into a class and terms with higher readability are needed.

3   Knowledge Work Lifelog Application

This section shows the overview of the proposed application to support reviewing and searching daily activities.

Fig. 1, Fig. 2, and Fig. 3 show snapshots of the proposed application. An example scenario of the application is as follows:

- A user works as usual with the logger application running as a background process. The logger application records user operation and sensor information. In this paper, we suppose a typical office work style with an Windows personal computer though this application supports Windows and Android platforms as written in [8].
- When the user wants to review the user's own activities about a specific day, he/she shows the lifelog viewer. Fig. 1 shows a screenshot of the viewer application. The user's lifelog events are shown in a timeline from top to bottom of the window. Each lifelog event includes the title of the activity, an icon indicating the kind of activity, the resources used, and tag terms for annotation. When the user

pushes one or more tags, the timeline is refined and only activities with these tags are shown. When the user inputs a query into the text box, specific events are searched. When the user clicks a resource name, the corresponding file or webpage is opened. If the system cannot find the file in the specific path, a desktop search application starts. When the user wants to review the user's own activities about a week, he/she can use the weekly view with pushing the 'W' button.

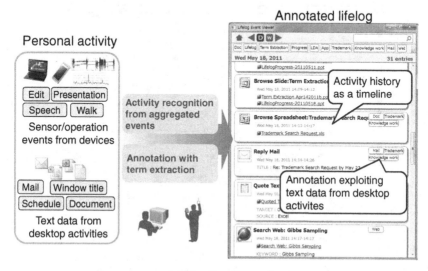

(a) Timeline view.

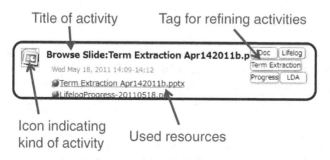

(b) Lifelog event in detail.

Fig. 1. Screenshot of lifelog viewer (timeline view)[1]

- If the user wants to see the user's activity in a more summarized view, he/she uses the monthly view in calendar style (Fig. 2). The calendar view shows the break-down of activity time per topic. Each topic title of topic is automatically extracted.

---

[1] In this paper, contents of each view are translated from Japanese. The same shall apply figures hereafter.

The method of topic title extraction is described below. If the user wants to know the detailed activity for a specific day, he/she selects the target day and opens the timeline view. The user can also define pattern matching rules for assigning specific activities to predefined categories. Pattern matching rules can be applied for extracted terms and activity types.

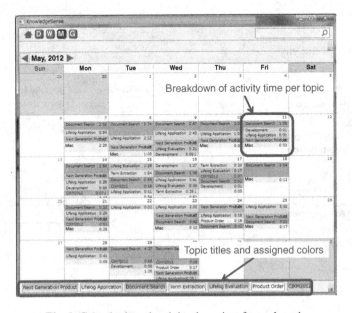

Fig. 2. Calendar-based activity time view for each topic

- If the user wants to know the summary of daily, weekly, or monthly activity time, he/she opens the graph view in bar chart style (Fig. 3). Application running time (including time when the user does not use the personal computer, such as suspended time), total actual work time, and work time for each topic are shown in the view.

Thus, our proposed system enables users to easily review their daily activities or refer to resources used in the past. Since all processes, i.e., recording activities, annotation, and topic classification, are automatically executed, the cost of using this system is low.

Especially, the views of Fig. 2 and Fig. 3 are implemented based on trial users of our previous version [8]. We had the one-month preliminary trial in our organization, and then collected opinions about requests for the application from 29 people. From their opinions, we found that visualization of activity statistics with monthly or weekly view is required.

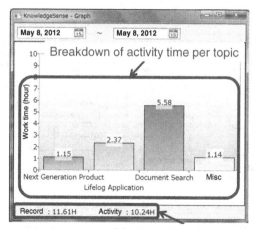

Fig. 3. Graph-based activity time view for each topic

4   System Overview

This section shows the overview and the process flow of the proposed method to support reviewing a knowledge work lifelog. Fig. 4 shows the flow of lifelog generation. The lifelogging method includes the following steps: lifelog event generation, annotation term extraction, topic title estimation, event merging and topic allocation, and event visualization. Since the first two steps are similar to the previous work [8], these steps are briefly described in this paper.

4.1   Lifelog Event Generation

Firstly, the logger application logs sensor events and operation events as a background process. Our system currently supports about 90 events for Windows and Android platforms. These events include operation events for desktop activities such as office document operations, web browsing, email operations, active window changes, and keyboard events. These events are input into the sensor event buffer. In our current system, sensor events detected on an Android terminal is merged to the events of a Windows PC by the import module.

Secondly, the lifelog event detection module generates lifelog events from combinations of sensor events in the sensor event buffer. For example, a lifelog event 'presentation' is generated from 'slideshow' and 'speech' sensor events. Our system currently supports about 40 lifelog events. Detected lifelog events are stored in the lifelog database.

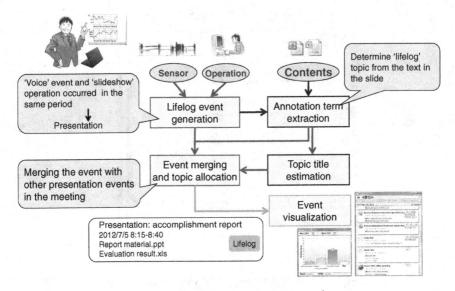

Fig. 4. Flow of lifelog generation

4.2   Annotation Term Extraction

This section describes the process flow of extracting terms used as annotation from the content database. To support review of knowledge work activities, annotation terms should be typical topic terms of a user's activities and interpretable for the user. In the proposed system, we combine LDA (latent Dirichlet allocation) [2] for extracting typical topic terms and C-value [3] calculation for extracting readable terms. Fig. 5 shows the annotation term extraction process. This process includes three steps: preprocess, important term estimation, and collocation extraction.

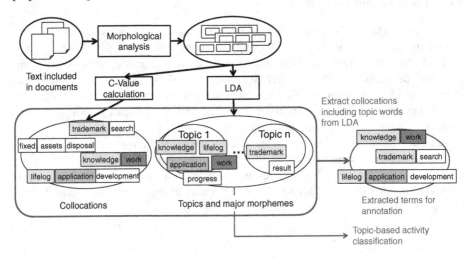

Fig. 5. Flow of annotation term extraction

Firstly, as preprocess, documents are converted into a series of morphemes by morphological analysis. We use MeCab [5] for the Japanese morphological analysis module. In the evaluation of this application described below, we used the Japanese version.

Secondly, LDA-based topic estimation is executed. LDA [2] is a language generation model that considers a set of documents as a mixture of latent topics. Each latent topic is a multinomial distribution with words. The parameter that controls the generation model of latent topics is expressed as a Dirichlet distribution, and words for each document are modeled with multinomial distribution. We use Collapsed Gibbs Sampling [4], [9] for the parameter estimation. We use a number of topics with the smallest perplexity after a hundred sampling iterations. Then, terms with higher occurrence probabilities for each topic are extracted as term candidates.

Thirdly, collocations are extracted with C-value calculation. An independent morpheme extracted with LDA does not have readability for a user to interpret the user's activities because of the small length. We use the C-Value [3] calculation technique as a readable collocation extraction method. A C-value for a collocation a is calculated as

$$Cvalue(a) = (length(a) - 1)\left(freq(a) - \frac{t(a)}{c(a)}\right),$$

where $t(a)$ means the occurrence frequency of longer collocations, and $c(a)$ means the number of these collocations.

Finally, collocations that have high C-value scores and include terms extracted through the LDA are extracted as annotation, as shown in Fig. 1.

The above steps are basically the same as in the previous work [8]. The same method is used as in the previous work, but, in addition, terms with lower probabilities are removed from the topic.

4.3   Topic Title Extraction

Furthermore, the collocation including the highest probability of occurrence in each topic, which means the characteristic term, is selected as the topic title. The set of terms for each topic is also stored. For each lifelog event, the system assigns a topic that includes terms of the topic in the event title or resource.

4.4   Event Merging and Topic Allocation

The duration of each lifelog event acquired in the previous section is too short as an activity history. Thus, activities in the same period of time are merged. In fact, we used the threshold of thirty minutes as the time distance, and the period of one lifelog event is up to 120 minutes. We used this threshold because each user can only remember each activity for a period of a certain duration, not one or five minutes.

For example, when a user edits a document referring to another document in a task, active applications are frequently changed. In this case, it is reasonable that both documents belong in the same task rather than that these documents are independent. Therefore, the same lifelog events in the same period of time and events in the same event categories, e.g., reading documents and editing documents, are merged into a lifelog event. Used resources and annotated tags of these events are also merged.

As a result, annotation terms and a topic are assigned for each lifelog event.

4.5   Event Visualization

Finally, the viewer application shows the activity history as Fig. 1, Fig. 2, and Fig. 3 based on lifelog events with tags and topics. The user reviews or searches their activity history with the timeline view, the calendar view, and the graph view.

5   Evaluation

We empirically investigated to what degree our annotation method satisfied users.

In advance, we let five subjects (knowledge workers in the IT domain) collect their lifelogs with their own personal computers for ten days. During this period, they worked in a normal way.

After this period, we collected 1,458 events related to our experiment. We had the subjects rate annotation terms, extracted topics and activity time output from the proposed system.

5.1   Extracted Annotation Terms

First, the system extracted up to twenty terms with the highest C-values for annotation. We used email titles, file names of Microsoft Office documents, and the text of the first page of these files for the input text after our preliminary investigation. Each subject rated annotations from the perspective of remindability, which means to what degree annotations remind users of concrete activities. This score indicates usefulness for reminding subjects of their activity histories at three levels: remindable (3); somewhat remindable (2); not remindable (1).

Fig. 6 shows average scores of individual users for n-best terms of C-value score. Average scores of all subjects for 5-best, 10-best, 15-best, and 20-best are 2.56, 2.4, 2.39, and 2.32, respectively.

From Fig. 6, we found that using extracted terms with higher C-values contributes to lifelog reviewing, although there is variability among subjects. On average, subjects were not bothered by noisy annotations with higher C-values.

Examples of 'not relevant' terms are as follows: collocation generation fault, e.g., 'For confirm 20120511' or ' "invited paper" "commentary" ', and too general terms for topic annotation, e.g., 'work description' or 'previous minutes.' These problems should be fixed in future.

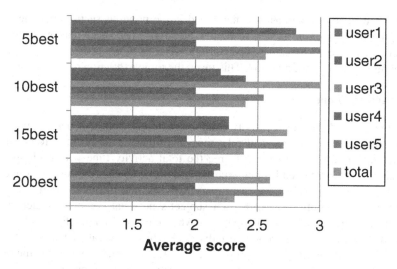

Fig. 6. Evaluation result for n-best annotation terms

5.2   Extracted Topics

Next, each subject rated relevance of extracted topic titles at three levels: relevant (3); somewhat relevant (2); not relevant (1).

Fig. 7 shows average scores of individual subjects for extracted topic titles. The numbers of topics the users 1-5 evaluated are 4, 7, 5, 6, and 3, respectively. The total number of topics is 25.

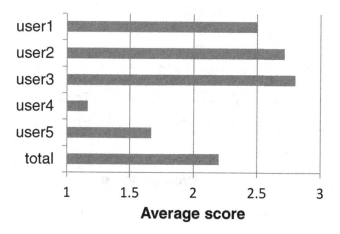

Fig. 7. Evaluation result for topic titles

From Fig. 7, we found that extracted terms are useful for topic title on average. However, there is greater variability among subjects than in the case of the evaluation results for extracted annotation terms. One reason is the term extraction problem, which is the same problem as that mentioned in the previous section. For the user 4, the degree of satisfaction is low in both evaluations. The other reason is the small number of documents for some subjects. For the user 5, the primary work was programming in the evaluation period. This made the topic extraction result worse.

5.3   Activity Time

The subjects rated their own activity time for each day from two perspectives: relevance of total activity time and relevance of primary activity time. Relevance of total activity time means to what degree the total activity time with each subject's personal computer matched his/her experience at three levels: relevant (3); somewhat (2); not relevant (1). Relevance of primary activity time means to what degree the primary topic's activity time with each subject's personal computer matched their experience at three levels: relevant (3); somewhat relevant (2); not relevant (1).

Fig. 8 shows the average scores of individual subjects for calculated activity time. From Fig. 8, total activity time is properly calculated to some extent. Since the ratings depend on how much each subject used applications that are compatible with our logger, long-term evaluation and evaluation considering each subject's work style are needed.

As to the primary activity time, our current method is not insufficient. Since calculating primary activity time adequately requires both good topic estimation and good activity time calculation, we should refine our methods.

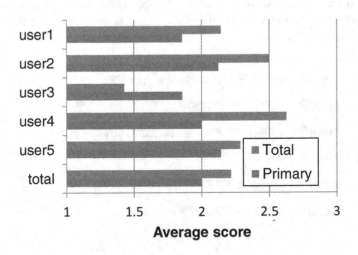

Fig. 8. Evaluation Result for daily activities

6   Conclusion

In this paper, we proposed a topic-based activity review application that supports knowledge workers in reviewing activity history, exploiting text data acquired from desktop activities. Our prototype system monitors a user's desktop activities after combining raw events, extracts possible annotation labels from documents and text data, extracts topic titles, and calculates activity time by each topic. According to an empirical evaluation with five subjects, we confirmed that the term extraction method is efficient for lifelog annotation and topic title extraction. We also identified challenges concerning determination of detailed activity time.

References

1. Bjellerup, P., Cama, K.J., Desikan, M., Guo, Y., Kale, A.G., Lai, J.C., Lethif, N., Lu, J., Topkara, M., Wissel, S.H.: FALCON: seamless access to meeting data from the inbox and calendar. In: 19th ACM Conference on Information and Knowledge Management (CIKM 2010), pp. 1951–1952. ACM, New York (2010)
2. Blei, D.M., Ng, A.Y., Jordan, M.I.: Latent dirichlet allocation. J. Mach. Learn. Res. 3, 993–1022 (2003)
3. Frantzi, K.T., Ananiadou, S.: Extracting nested collocations. In: The 16th International Conference on Computational Linguistics (COLING 1996), vol. 1, pp. 41–46. Association for Computational Linguistics, Stroudsburg (1996)
4. Griffiths, T., Steyvers, M.: Finding Scientific Topics. Proc. Natl. Acad. Sci. USA 101, 5228–5235 (2004)
5. Kudo, T., Yamamoto, K., Matsumoto, Y.: Appliying Conditional Random Fields to Japanese Morphological Analysis. In: 2004 Conference on Empirical Methods in Natural Language Processing (EMNLP 2004), Barcelona, Spain, pp. 230–237 (2004)
6. Mirza, H.T., Chen, L., Chen, G., Hussain, I., He, X.: Switch Detector: An Activity Spotting System for Desktop. In: 20th ACM Conference on Information and Knowledge Management (CIKM 2011), pp. 2285–2288. ACM, New York (2011)
7. Okamoto, M., Iketani, N., Nishimura, K., Kikuchi, M., Cho, K., Hattori, M.: Finding two-level interpersonal context: proximity and conversation detection from personal audio feature data. In: 9th Annual Conference of the International Speech Communication Association (Interspeech 2008), Brisbane, Australia, pp. 2482–2485 (2008)
8. Okamoto, M., Watanabe, N., Nagano, S., Cho, K.: Annotating Knowledge Work Lifelog: Term Extraction from Sensor and Operation History. In: 20th ACM Conference on Information and Knowledge Management (CIKM 2011), pp. 2581–2584. ACM, New York (2011)
9. Porteous, I., Newman, D., Ihler, A., Asuncion, A., Smyth, P., Welling, M.: Fast collapsed gibbs sampling for latent dirichlet allocation. In: 14th ACM SIGKDD International Conference on Knowledge Discovery and Data Mining (KDD 2008), pp. 569–577. ACM, New York (2008)
10. Shen, J., Irvine, J., Bao, X., Goodman, M., Kolibaba, S., Tran, A., Carl, F., Kirschner, B., Stumpf, S., Dietterich, T.G.: Detecting and correcting user activity switches: algorithms and interfaces. In: 14th International Conference on Intelligent User Interfaces (IUI 2009), pp. 117–126. ACM, New York (2009)

The Use of Token-Based Protocols in CSCW Tasks – An Empirical Examination

Christopher G. Harris

Computer Science Department, SUNY Oswego, Oswego, NY 13126
christopher.harris@oswego.edu

Abstract. In Computer Supported Cooperative Work (CSCW), many tasks require exclusive access to a shared resource by a single collaborator. Similarly, in distributed systems, mutual exclusion is required to ensure concurrency in a resource shared among several processes. These resource allocation algorithms can be divided into two genres: token-based and permission-based. To date, few empirical studies have evaluated token-based collaborative behavior in CSCW tasks. We examine four token-based protocols on a task which requires participants to properly order a series of screenshots obtained from ten short films. Using teams of 3, 4, and 5 participants who are collectively incentivized to perform the task as quickly as possible, we evaluate the effects of team size and token based protocol on task completion and participant satisfaction across 600 sessions. Our study determined that task satisfaction was negatively correlated with team size and positively correlated with the perception of "fairness", or lack of potential bias, of each protocol.

1   Introduction

The use of purely virtual teams is growing. A 2012 RW3 CultureWizard survey of 3300 employees in 103 countries found that 87 percent of respondents belonged to a virtual team and 41 percent of these respondents had never met their teammates face-to-face [16]. Those who manage virtual teams have challenges that often differ from those who handle face-to-face teams, such as a heavier reliance on collaborative communication tools to interact. When virtual teams are static, teammates become aware of the strengths and weaknesses of their fellow collaborators and trust is established [2, 3]. However, with the increase in the use of semi-anonymous freelancers on websites like eLance[1] and Freelancer[2], the nature of virtual work frequently comprises ad hoc teams brought together to examine a specific problem or work on a specific task, and is temporary by design [12]. The use of temporary work teams are anticipated to increase in the next decade and beyond due to a number of favorable factors, including more efficient virtual access to experts through advances in communication tools, a growing disparity in employment costs between the developed and the developing world, and the ease of transmitting payments across the globe

---

[1] http://www.elance.com
[2] http://www.freelancer.com

T. Yuizono et al. (Eds.): CollabTech 2014, CCIS 460, pp. 40–53, 2014.
© Springer-Verlag Berlin Heidelberg 2014

[14, 21]. This virtual team approach to accomplishing ad hoc tasks has some short-comings; as indicated in the 2012 RW3 CultureWizard survey, common problems encountered with virtual teams are that they fail to provide suffi-cient time to build relationships, require speedy decision making due to time zone differences, involve working with colleagues who do not actively participate, and require integration of different leadership and decision making styles. Naturally, these obstacles raise issues of trust; Jarvenpaa and Liedner investigated how trust develops in temporary virtual teams [10]. When faced with short deadlines and no face-to-face time to establish trust, the team members relied on expectations of trust from other settings that were familiar to them. However, virtual teams with low levels of initial trust and no actions to affirm trust continue to operate in a low-trust environment, which Jarvenpaa and Liedner found negatively impacted the team's performance.

It is therefore important to identify protocols that encourage efficiency by small virtual teams who have little or no previous working knowledge with each other. Dis-tributed algorithms that provide mutual exclusive access to a shared resource, which we discuss in the next section, may provide some guidance. However, unlike ma-chines, humans need some inducement to perform at their best. Thus, one approach to the rapid alignment of teams is to offer a team-based incentive. As with conven-tional teams, incentives that depend on team performance can play a role in aligning team members toward a specific goal [9]. However, some researchers have found that team-based rewards can also reduce motivation, particularly for more expe-rienced team members [4]. In our study, we use team-based incentives for a task where each participant has an equal opportunity to contribute and examine if extrinsic incentives are effective in aligning collaborators toward a team-based goal.

The remainder of this paper is organized as follows. In the next section, we dis-cuss the background and motivation behind our experiments. In Section 3, we pro-vide a description of our experimental methods. In Section 4, we provide our results. Section 5 provides some additional analysis and is followed by a discussion of our general findings. We conclude and briefly discuss future directions of our work in Section 6.

2   Background and Motivation

Although the number of empirical studies in CSCW is limited, there are parallels with machine-based distributed systems, which we describe in this section.

2.1   Experiments with Virtual Teams

Despite the growth of ad hoc virtual teams over the last decade, there have been only few studies that have touched on collaboration in such environments; moreover, these have been focused on other aspects of task coordination rather than the protocols em-ployed. Morris and Paepke performed a token-based study called Teamsearch using a tabletop device [13], but its examination of token passing and team size was not explored. Antle et. al. performed an empirical study on sustainable development using tokens in [1], but the focus was on sustainability, not on different mechanisms on concurrency. We found no other empirical examples in the CSCW literature examining the effectiveness of token-based protocols or number of collaborators.

2.2   Similarity with Mutually Exclusion Algorithms

One of the most studied areas in distributed systems is mutual exclusion (Mutex), where processes communicate by asynchronous message passing to coordinate mutually exclusive access to resources. These resource allocation algorithms, first introduced by Dijkstra   [5], share a number of similarities with coordinating access among virtual human teams. First, machine processes and human collaborators can be considered as agents, and the motivation for each must be understood. In some cases, trust is unknown for each agent and cannot be assumed. Second, each protocol must determine the order in which agent (human or machine) can access a specific resource.   Third, both protocols must handle issues of starvation, race conditions, and bias between participants. Last, both types of agents are evaluated on the same metrics, namely speed and task accuracy.

Broadly speaking, these Mutex algorithms can be divided into two families: *permission-based* and *token-based*. Permission-based algorithms, which typically require additional communication between each collaborator when permission to access a resource is required, are best suited for systems with infrequent demand for a resource; token-based systems, in which a privilege message, or *token*, is shared among all processes in a system (or collaborators in a task), are better suited to systems with resources that are in high demand. Furthermore, another advantage of token-based systems, unlike permission-based systems, is that they rely on a unique token and thus are deadlock-free. In our study, we limit our evaluation to token-based systems.

Token-based systems can be further divided into two different genres: *centralized* and *decentralized*. Centralized systems have a single decision maker that determines which process or collaborator has access to the token (and thus the resource), but may become a bottleneck if the token is not adequately managed. Centralized systems may also suffer from bias towards or against a particular collaborator, potentially leading to starvation. We examine one centralized system as part of our study. On the other hand, decentralized systems provide an established set of rules to determine which collaborator gets the token and which collaborator(s) must wait. Implicit and explicit token-based systems are described in more detail in [6].

Although a number of decentralized algorithms have been established in resource allocation, e.g., [18-20], we examine three that show the most promise for applying to human collaboration tasks: *time based*, where token requests are queued in the order they are requested, *last user determined*, where a token is sent from the current collaborator (user) to another collaborator based on the current token holder's sole decision, and *round robin*, where the token is sent in an established pattern (usually clockwise or counter-clockwise) between all collaborators who have made a request for the token.

Protocols can be *explicit*, with a predefined turn-taking rules, as with the time based and round robin protocols or *implicit*, where the freedom of choice can be made by a collaborator, as with the last user determined protocol and the centralized protocol.

We found no studies in the literature which have empirically compared these centralized and decentralized protocols for virtual teams in CSCW. Dommel and Garcia-Luna-Aceves describe a concept called floor control in [6] which is a temporary permission to access a specific resource; however, they do not conduct any empirical studies on their methods. Prasad et. al. describe an empirical study on floor control in [15], but their objective of their study is different from the one we examine here. Our objective is to obtain a better understanding of which token-based protocols work best for improving the performance of small teams. We measure this by the time taken to perform a task and by a self-reported collaborator satisfaction score. A better understanding of which protocol to use in a given situation can lead to better team performance and greater team satisfaction, particularly when teams are newly established or temporary in nature.

Our contributions are fourfold. First, we empirically examine different token-based systems with different numbers of randomly-assigned collaborators in a task in which each collaborator has an equal opportunity to contribute. This equal opportunity condition allows us to observe the contention between participants for a single resource. Second, in addition to measuring the amount of time taken to complete a task, we also measure each participant's satisfaction with the collaboration protocol. This metric gives us an opportunity to evaluate the perception of fairness, even when there is no evidence that any bias has actually occurred. Third, because ad hoc collaborators need to be quickly aligned towards a single objective, we provide an extrinsic incentive in the form of a monetary bonus for those teams who are able to complete the task quickly and accurately. Last, we examine demographic information obtained from the collaborators and examine if collaboration systems are favored by certain groups of people.

2.3 Research Questions

We examine the following research questions.

1. Are there any main or interaction effects with number of collaborators on task satisfaction?
2. Are there any main or interaction effects with type of token-based protocol on (a) time taken or on (b) task satisfaction?
3. Do demographics impact the task satisfaction of a given protocol?

3 Experimental Methods

To study collaborator behavior among ad hoc teams, we wanted a task that was easy to understand, provided no single collaborator with a specific advantage, and which could be easily measured. We developed a game that allowed us to examine two different factors: token-based approach (centralized, round robin, last-user determined, or time-based) and number of collaborators (3, 4 or 5).

3.1   Experimental Setup

We developed a game that required participants to complete a task in small groups. For each task, called a *session*, the type of token management was randomly assigned. Since most players participated in multiple sessions, participants were provided a new identity for each session. This reduced the possibility that any disagreements between collaborators in one session would carry over to future sessions. Each collaborator could only participate once for each short film, or in a maximum of 10 sessions.

We examined our factors across 10 short films found on YouTube; each film was between 3.5 to 8.5 minutes in length, with an average length of 5.5 minutes. These short films were selected through a poll conducted on Amazon Mechanical Turk (MTurk)[3] prior to the commencement of our study. Twenty screenshots, called tiles, were taken from each short film, with considerable care taken so that the tiles could not be ambiguously ordered and that the tiles were associated with significant events in each short film.

Four tiles were randomly distributed to each collaborator (e.g., groups of 3 collaborators were assigned a total of 3 x 4 = 12 tiles; groups of 4 collaborators were assigned a total of 4 x 4 = 16 tiles). Participants watched the assigned short film and were then instructed to collaborate with others to order all assigned tiles in the same order as the short film. Participants could only add their own assigned tiles to the ordered list, called a *storyboard*, when they had possession of the token. Because each collaborator could only see the tiles assigned to him or her and those already added to the storyboard, no single participant could direct others on when or where to place their assigned tiles; each participant had to rely on efficient assignment of the token in order for the team to obtain a low time. Participants could type messages to each other using a simple messaging service. A session timer was started when all participants had finished watching the short film and a token was randomly assigned to one participant. The timer ended when all tiles were put in the correct order and at least one of the collaborators hit a "submit answer" button. The films used in our study and the URLs for each are provided in Table 1.

Table 1. Title, length and URL of each of the short films examined in our study, and the user rating obtained in a pilot study (10 = best, 1 = worst)

Film Title	Length	URL	User Rating
Lovefield	5:29	https://www.youtube.com/watch?v=4meeZifCVro	9.07
The Elevator	3:37	https://www.youtube.com/watch?v=Q-TQQE1y68c	8.87
My Shoes	3:54	https://www.youtube.com/watch?v=Y_F4-hV0iPM	8.80
Inbox	8:37	https://www.youtube.com/watch?v=75wNgCo-BQM	8.69
Pigeon: Impossible	6:14	https://www.youtube.com/watch?v=jEjUAnPc2VA	8.47
The Exam	7:00	https://www.youtube.com/watch?v=1HC1ANf4L6s	8.20
Fireflies	5:53	https://www.youtube.com/watch?v=1d_mCmMdLIY	8.07
The Date	3:48	https://www.youtube.com/watch?v=t7PQJ2yyIvI	8.00
Carrot Crazy	3:28	https://www.youtube.com/watch?v=7V7MOk0FZrg	7.93
Thirst	6:30	https://www.youtube.com/watch?v=ck0028dgUmA	7.87

---

[3] http://www.mturk.com

3.2   Assigning Participants to Sessions

The single-greatest challenge we faced in our game design was the ability to queue 3-5 players to be available at the same time to play a synchronous game. We eventually resolved this issue using a slightly modified version of TurkServer [11] to queue participants until we had the necessary number of players available. Even with this queuing method in place, the attrition rate in our study was 17.9 percent, illustrating the challenges of multi-player synchronous games.

Our study was conducted between June 2, 2013 and October 15, 2013. Participants were initially solicited through MTurk and via word-of-mouth and were paid US $0.10 to provide demographic information (age, gender, self-reported location), to participate in a session, and to provide satisfaction on the protocol used for that session. We recorded their IP address to verify their self-reported location, and did not include participants in our demographic evaluation if the locations differed.

Participants could be assigned to different token-based protocols for each of the 10 sessions, but they would always be assigned teams with the same number of collaborators. A total of 784 unique players participated, representing an average of 3.18 sessions per player. Separate leaderboards were maintained for each combination of token-based protocol and number of collaborators, for a total of 12 leaderboards. Collaborators were told that they (along with their team) would be entered in a drawing for a $20 cash bonus provided their session was listed on the leaderboard at the end of our study. This incentive appeared to motivate a number of participants to play as much as possible, as nearly a third of all collaborators played the maximum of 10 sessions. Participants in the 3-collaborator models had a higher retention rate than those in the 4 or 5 collaborator models. Nearly a third (32.6%) of all participants played the maximum of 10 sessions, which is a far higher retention rate than typical for repeated tasks conducted through crowdsourcing (e.g., [7, 8, 17]). This indicates the monetary incentives we offered worked well and the task provided was sufficiently engaging. The distribution of number of sessions per player is provided in Figure 1.

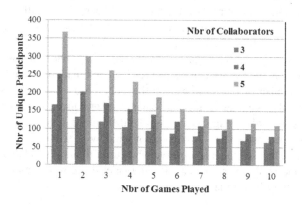

Fig. 1. Participant retention rate used in this study, broken down by number of collaborators

3.3   Game Interface

The game interface used in our study was made available to participants through a unique link for each of the 600 sessions we conducted. Once the participant clicked on the session link, they entered a queue and waited for the right number of participants to arrive. Queuing time ranged from a few seconds to several minutes.

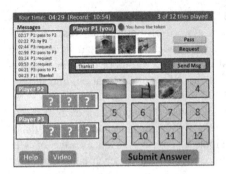 

Fig. 2. Examples of the game screens for the three-collaborator version (left) and the five-collaborator version (right) for the time-based protocol. On the left, the participant currently has the token whereas on the right, another participant has the token.

Next, the participant is provided with the rules for the assigned token-based protocol and the URL for the short film. After they complete viewing of the short film, the participant clicks a button and waits for the other participants. Figure 2 provides two examples of the game screens provided to each participant with the version with three collaborators on the left and the version with five collaborators on the right (the version with four collaborators is not shown due to space).

At the top of each participant's game screen, they are provided a status bar containing the elapsed time, the best time recorded for the combination of number of collaborators, and the number of tiles currently on the storyboard. Below the status bar, the four tiles randomly assigned to the participant are provided, along with buttons to pass and request the token. Figure 3 shows the different participant areas for each of the four token-based protocols. A messaging window is given to communicate with the other users. The user can also observe who currently has the token along with the other token requests along the lower left-hand side of the screen and the storyboard along the lower right-hand side of the screen.

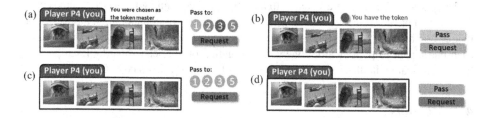

Fig. 3. Examples of options available to the participant for passing and requesting tokens for our four protocols: (a) centralized (b) time-based, (c) last user determined and (d) round robin

In order to place one of their four assigned tiles on the storyboard (or to rearrange tiles already played by other participants on the storyboard), the token is required to be in their possession. Therefore only one participant can interact with the storyboard at any one time. The protocols used are:

1. *Centralized* – One randomly assigned participant is randomly assigned the token and they are given the task to send and request the token for all other participants for the entire session.
2. *Time Based (decentralized)* – One participant is initially assigned the token by random determination. Other participants who wish to obtain the token can request the token by pressing the "request" button. The token requests are processed in chronological order based on the time the button was pressed.
3. *Last User Determined (decentralized)* – One participant is initially assigned the token by random determination. Each participant, when they have possession of the token, can explicitly send the token to any other participant, but they do not have the ability to revoke the token from other participants.
4. *Round Robin (decentralized)* – One participant is initially assigned the token by random determination. Once a participant passes the token, token travels in a circular order until it reaches the next participant that has made a token request.

Participants can view the short film in another window by pressing a view button at the bottom left of the game screen. Also at the bottom left of the screen, there is a help button that provides the rules given to each participant at the beginning of the game.

The timer stops once all the tiles are in the correct order on the storyboard and a "submit answer" button below the storyboard (on the bottom right of the screen) has been pressed by one of the participants. Participants are not told which tiles are incorrectly ordered, but a count of incorrectly ordered tiles is provided to all participants once the "submit answer" button has been pressed. The "submit answer" button remains greyed out and unavailable until all tiles have been placed on the storyboard. Once the user has submitted their work, they are asked the following question:

```
On the task you have just completed, how satisfied were you on
the fairness on the sharing of the token?  (1 = extremely dissa-
tisfied, 10 = extremely satisfied).
```

The participant is then presented with a leaderboard containing the top 10 team scores for that combination of token-based protocol and number of collaborators, along with a unique combination of four letters and numbers for that session. A link was provided to each participant to periodically review their standing on the leaderboard. Each participant on the team with the lowest time at the end of our study was paid $20.

4   Results

The mean and standard deviation for the time taken and the average task satisfaction rating from 600 sessions is presented in Table 2. From these results, we can observe that the task time increases and the task satisfaction decreases as the number of collaborators in the task increase from three to five. Additionally, the round robin protocol results in higher task completion times regardless of the number of contributors used, while the time-based protocol results in the shortest completion times. For tasks with fewer collaborators, the time-based protocol results in higher task satisfaction scores, but as the number of collaborators grow to five, it becomes the protocol with the lowest task satisfaction score. We address this issue further in the discussion section.

Table 2. Mean and standard deviations for time taken and average satisfaction rating for each factor (number of collaborators, protocol used)

	Time (seconds)		Avg. Satisfaction Rating		
Factor	μ	SD	μ	SD	N
Number of Collaborators					
3	788.6	71.1	7.70	0.81	200
4	1037.8	95.4	7.75	0.81	200
5	1261.3	98.7	6.85	0.90	200
Protocol Used					
Centralized	1008.2	86.3	7.68	0.86	150
Time-based	996.8	85.6	7.61	0.75	150
Last User Determined	1021.9	72.8	7.60	0.76	150
Round Robin	1090.0	108.9	6.83	1.00	150
Number of Collaborators ×					
Protocol Used					
3, Centralized	767.0	63.1	7.89	0.91	50
3, Time-based	757.4	55.8	8.20	0.48	50
3, Last User Determined	783.4	70.2	7.73	0.82	50
3, Round Robin	846.4	95.3	6.99	1.03	50
4, Centralized	1019.3	100.7	7.95	0.92	50
4, Time-based	1008.0	97.6	8.24	0.48	50
4, Last User Determined	1024.2	74.7	7.77	0.82	50
4, Round Robin	1099.8	108.6	7.02	1.03	50
5, Centralized	1238.2	95.1	7.22	0.75	50
5, Time-based	1225.0	103.4	6.39	1.29	50
5, Last User Determined	1258.0	73.6	7.30	0.63	50
5, Round Robin	1323.9	122.7	6.49	0.95	50

A two-way ANOVA was conducted that examined the effect of the number of collaborators and token-based protocol on the *time taken* to perform the task. The results are provided in Table 3. Although no significant interaction effect was found, the simple main effects of the number of collaborators, $F (2, 588) = 1364.548$, $p < .0001$, as well as with the protocol used $F (3, 588) = 32.023$, $p < .0001$, were both significant. It is expected that as the number of collaborators participating increases, the time taken also increases, since the size of the storyboard increases as well. However, the effect of the protocol used on time to perform the task answers part (a) of our second hypothesis and we find protocol does have a simple main effect on the time taken.

A two-way ANOVA was also conducted to examine the effect of the number of collaborators and token-based protocol on the average task satisfaction rating. Simple main effects were found for the number of collaborators, $F (2, 588) = 67.503$, $p < .0001$, as well as with the protocol used $F (3, 588) = 31.743$, $p < .0001$. An interaction effect between the two factors were also found, $F (6 588) = 9.229$, $p < .0001$. This addresses our first hypotheses and part (b) of our second hypothesis. We find that both the number of collaborators and the protocol used does have an effect on task satisfaction rating.

The relationship between the task satisfaction rating and the time taken for the task was strong, particularly for tasks with three or four collaborators, as shown in Figure 4. As the number of collaborators on a task increases, the task satisfaction rating decreases but the number of collaborators becomes a weaker overall predictor for task satisfaction.

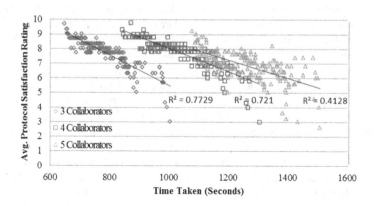

Fig. 4. Relationship between the time taken and the average task satisfaction rating for tasks with 3, 4 and 5 contributors. The R-squared value is given for tasks with different collaborator sizes.

5   Analysis and Discussion

In Figure 5, we examine how our two factors interact for each of our 600 sessions. We break each of the different collaboration sizes (our first factor) into different graphs and examine the average task satisfaction rating (our second factor) as it relates to the time taken.

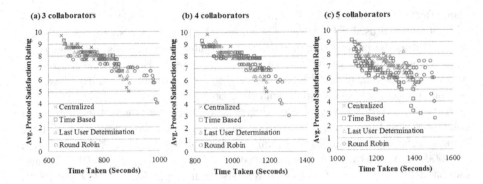

Fig. 5. Illustration of task satisfaction rating and time taken for each token based protocol, broken into separate graphs by number of collaborators

We observe that clustering is still fairly cohesive based on the token-based protocol used; however, as the number of collaborators increases from three (left-most graph) to five (right-most graph), the clustering becomes less cohesive. This indicates that the time taken becomes a weaker predictor of the task satisfaction and other factors, particularly the protocol used may become a better predictor. We also notice that the round robin protocol is our consistently weakest performer whereas the time based protocol is a strong performer when the number of contributors used is three or four, but a poor performer when the number of contributors increases to five. We logged information on each of the 600 sessions, including the messaging between participants, and therefore we infer some reasons why this may be the case. First, many participants in the five-collaborator model using the time-based protocol were requesting the token as soon as possible but took considerable time to play their tiles. Much like a contestant on a game show who presses the response button in order to "jump the queue" before listening to the complete question, these participants were requesting the token before they were prepared to take action, frustrating others who were prepared but further down in the queue. This gave the impression that the protocol was being manipulated by some players, lowering that protocol's satisfaction rating. We did not observe this behavior in the models with three or four collaborators.

We were also surprised to see that the centralized protocol obtained better times than the last-user selection protocol (since both are implicit, we had initially anticipated them to have similar times). From the logged messages passed between participants, we see that if one participant is identified as the "token master", they are quicker to respond to token requests made by the other participants, whereas the participant in the last user determination model frequently took longer to pass the token, even when it had been requested by many players. The task satisfaction rating for the centralized model was lower than that of the last user determined protocol, however. This appeared to be skewed by participants in a few sessions; in those sessions, we observed there was an implication that two participants were passing between each other and ignoring all other participants. This implies that bonds between collaborators could be identified and established quickly. This phenomenon was not observed in the centralized model.

We recorded the self-reported demographics of each participant, including age range, gender and location. This gave us some insight into how the task satisfaction rating of each protocol was affected by demographics. We broke geographic locations into seven regions and three age groups, which is given in Table 3. We performed chi-squared tests on the ratings each participant provided.

Overall, we find region do have preferences, χ^2 (6, N=776) = 262.883, p < 0.0001; task satisfaction ratings for the explicit models (time based and round robin) were higher for participants from Europe, North America and Australia, whereas implicit models (centralized and last player determined) were favored by participants from South Asia, South and Central America and Africa and the Middle East. The centralized protocol was favored more by females, χ^2 (3, N=321) = 170.833, p < 0.0001, and by participants over 35 years of age χ^2 (3, N=154) = 112.40, p < 0.0001, whereas the time-based protocol was favored by males χ^2 (3, N=455) = 211.54, p < 0.0001, and by participants under 25 years of age, χ^2 (3, N=303) = 89.481, p < 0.0001. We therefore find that the protocol used does matter for task satisfaction for different geographic regions, genders and age groups. This reinforces our third hypotheses. We plan to explore the relationship between these demographic factors and protocol preferences in future work.

Table 3. Demographic breakdown of participants by region, gender and age range

	Female	Male	N
Region			
Africa and Middle East	6	37	43
Australia and Oceana	13	12	25
East and North Asia	18	29	47
Europe	73	69	142
North America	106	90	196
South and Central America	16	37	53
South Asia	89	181	270
TOTAL	**321**	**455**	**776**
Age Range			
Under 25	141	162	303
25-34	120	199	319
35 and Over	60	94	154
TOTAL	**321**	**455**	**776**

6   Conclusion

The number of tasks incorporating virtual collaborations is expected to increase due to favorable conditions in the global workplace. A large percentage of these collaborations will be short-term by nature, which means trust and bonding exercises between collaborators are not practical. In tasks where collaborators must compete for limited a limited set of resources, factors such as bias, concurrency, and deadlocking need to be adequately addressed. Thus, the mutual exclusion protocol and the size of the collaboration teams, when appropriately chosen, can contribute to task success.

An empirical study with 600 different tasks and 2400 participants was conducted that examined these two factors. We designed a game that had participants collaborate in a synchronous task of different sizes and different token-based protocols, four of which we borrow from work in distributed systems. The game used incentives to have participants work on a task to put screenshots of a short film in order on a storyboard. The task was designed to be easy to learn and require no prior external knowledge to participate. Providing monetary incentives aligned teams to focus on a single metric (task completion time) and as a result, our participant retention rate was much higher than expected, with a third of participants completing the maximum number of tasks available.

We explored several hypotheses in this study. We found that the time taken does depend on the protocol chosen. We also found that the self-reported task satisfaction rating depends on the time taken by the team to complete a task and the protocol used, with an overall preference for the time-based protocol in smaller groups and for the last user determined and centralized protocols in the larger collaboration model. In future work, we hope to expand our evaluation to larger groups to see if what we observed with the five-collaborator model follows a trend or if it was an anomaly.

Since worker satisfaction in these collaboration models correlates highly with greater trust between participants, the choice of protocol can enhance the collaborator effort or detract from it. This is particularly true early in the collaboration process when each participant has little information to use to determine trust, as Jarvenpaa and Leidner had illustrated in an earlier study [10].

Demographics also play a part in satisfaction with the protocol employed, with some regions of the world preferring implicit models (centralized and last user determined) while other regions prefer explicit models, particularly time-based protocols. Females and younger users gave higher task satisfaction scores using the centralized protocol whereas males and younger participants were happier with the time-based protocol; however, we realize the role of demographic in virtual task design needs to be examined in more detail.

In future work, we plan to study the role of communication in token passing, specifically we wish to see if a participant's satisfaction was related more to familiarity with the token-passing protocol than on the protocol's performance. We also plan to examine additional token-based protocols and examine the role of bias in collaborative tasks.

References

1. Antle, A.N., Bevans, A., Tanenbaum, J., Seaborn, K., Wang, S.: Futura: design for collaborative learning and game play on a multi-touch digital tabletop. In: Proceedings of the Fifth International Conference on Tangible, Embedded, and Embodied Interaction, pp. 93–100. ACM (January 2011)
2. Armstrong, D.J., Cole, P.: Managing distances and differences in geographically distributed work groups. In: Distributed Work, pp. 167–186 (2002)
3. Binder, J.C.: Global project management: communication, collaboration and management across borders. Gower Publishing, Ltd. (2007)
4. DeMatteo, J.S., Eby, L.T., Sundstrom, E.: Team-based rewards: current emiprical evidence. Research in Organizational Behavior 20, 141–183 (1998)

5. Dijkstra, E.W.: Cooperating Sequential Processes, Technical Report EWD-123 (1965)
6. Dommel, H.P., Garcia-Luna-Aceves, J.J.: Floor control for multimedia conferencing and collaboration. Multimedia Systems 5(1), 23–38 (1997)
7. Eickhoff, C., Harris, C.G., de Vries, A.P., Srinivasan, P.: Quality through flow and immersion: gamifying crowdsourced relevance assessments. In: Proceedings of the 35th International ACM SIGIR Conference on Research and Development in Information Retrieval, pp. 871–880. ACM (August 2012)
8. Harris, C., Wu, C.: Using tri-reference point theory to evaluate risk attitude and the effects of financial incentives in a gamified crowdsourcing task. Journal of Business Economics 84(3), 281–302 (2014)
9. Hertel, G., Geister, S., Konradt, U.: Managing virtual teams: A review of current empirical research. Human Resource Management Review 15(1), 69–95 (2005)
10. Jarvenpaa, S.L., Leidner, D.E.: Communication and trust in global virtual teams. Journal of Computer-Mediated Communication 3(4) (1998)
11. Mao, A., Chen, Y., Gajos, K.Z., Parkes, D., Procaccia, A.D., Zhang, H.: Turkserver: Enabling synchronous and longitudinal online experiments. In: Proceedings of HCOMP, vol. 12 (2012)
12. Mettler, A., Williams, A.D.: The rise of the micro-multinational: How freelancers and technology-savvy start-ups are driving growth, jobs and innovation. Lisbon Council Policy Brief 5(3) (2011)
13. Morris, M.R., Paepcke, A., Winograd, T.: Teamsearch: Comparing techniques for co-present collaborative search of digital media. In: Horizontal Interactive Human-Computer Systems. IEEE (January 2006)
14. Passerini, K., El Tarabishy, A., Patten, K.: The Changing Nature of "Workspace" and "Workplace:" What It Means for SMEs. In: Information Technology for Small Business, pp. 37–46. Springer, New York (2012)
15. Prasad, R.V., Jamadagni, H.S., Shankar, H.N., Pawelczak, P.: Fixing Number of Floors for Virtual Voice-Only Conference-an Empirical Study. In: International Symposium on Multimedia, pp. 120–127. IEEE Computer Society (December 2005)
16. RW3-CultureWizard. The Challenges of Working in Virtual Teams RW3-CultureWizard (2012), http://rw-3.com/2012VirtualTeamsSurveyReport.pdf
17. Rzeszotarski, J.M., Chi, E., Paritosh, P., Dai, P.: Inserting Micro-Breaks into Crowdsourcing Workflows. In: First AAAI Conference on Human Computation (March 2013)
18. Singh, M., Tapaswi, S.: Token Based Mutual Exclusion in Peer-to-Peer Systems. In: Technologies and Protocols for the Future of Internet Design: Reinventing the Web, pp. 214–228 (2012)
19. Singhal, M.: A heuristically-aided algorithm for mutual exclusion in distributed systems. IEEE Transactions on Computers 38(5), 651–662 (1989)
20. Suzuki, I., Kasami, T.: A distributed mutual exclusion algorithm. ACM Transactions on Computer Systems (TOCS) 3(4), 344–349 (1985)
21. Thissen, M.R., Myers, S.K., Sikes, R.N., Robinson, J.P., Grouverman, V.M.: Globalization of Software Development Teams. In: Pachura, P. (ed.) The Systemic Dimension of Globalization. InTech (2011), http://www.intechopen.com/books/the-systemic-dimension-of-globalization/globalization-of-software-development-teams

Effects of Gamification
on Electronic Brainstorming Systems

Takaya Yuizono, Quinzhe Xing, and Hiroaki Furukawa

Japan Advanced Institute of Science and Technology
1-1 Asahidai Nomi, Ishikawa 923-1211, Japan
yuizono@jaist.ac.jp

Abstract. This paper describes an electronic brainstorming system using gamification elements and examines three categories of fun. For this study, the elements of gamification are identified as: level up for hard fun, score for easy fun, leader board for people fun, gift for people fun, and badge for various forms of fun (hard, easy, and people fun). This study conducted several 30-minute experimental sessions using the designed brainstorming system. The results showed that the gamification element was the most effective catalyst to improving the quality of ideas of participants in terms of fluency, flexibility, and originality. By contrast, the study found no significant difference between results generated from cooperative gamification and those from competitive gamification.

Keywords: groupware, creativity, brainstorming, gamification.

1 Introduction

The creative power of people is considered by many companies to be a competitive resource in the development of innovative ideas, materials, services, and activities. Techniques related to the generation of ideas have been used in such organizations. The most popular is the brainstorming method proposed by Osborn [1]. This group method has been supported by other research for its effectiveness.

Social psychologists have confirmed through laboratory experiments that brainstorming conducted in groups is inferior to that which uses a pool of individuals. This is called a nominal group technique (NGT) [2]. However, electronic brainstorming [3], or what is known as the brain-writing technique [4], can produce similar results to those of NGT. Moreover, brainstorming is recognized as a part of daily practice at design firms such as IDEO [5].

In addition, gamification, which is a technique that introduces game concepts to nongaming tasks, has been praised as an effective method of motivating people to solve problems [6]. Researchers in organizational learning believe that social gaming environments may become major learning communities in the 21st century [7].

In this study, we apply gamification to electronic brainstorming and implement three categories of fun (hard, easy, and people fun) [8], [9] as gamification features in the design of an electronic brainstorming system. The paper then describes experiments conducted as well as evaluation methods, and results.

T. Yuizono et al. (Eds.): CollabTech 2014, CCIS 460, pp. 54–61, 2014.
© Springer-Verlag Berlin Heidelberg 2014

2   Gamification and Four Categories of Fun

Gamification is a technique that introduces gaming elements to many nongaming activities. Gamification has been formally defined as "the process of game-thinking and game mechanics to engage users and solve problems" [7]. For example, point card systems used by stores and other commercial establishments involve buyers collecting purchase points as a motivational means to encourage them to become repeat customers.

The four categories of fun proposed by Lazaro are based on four emotions typically encountered during game playing. The four categories of fun are labeled *easy fun*, *hard fun*, *people fun*, and *serious fun* [8], [9].

Easy fun stimulates user interest in novelty through exploration, role playing, and creativity. Hard fun stimulates user desire for challenge through the achievement of a difficult goal. People fun stimulates a user's love of friendship by means of competition or cooperation. Serious fun stimulates user's sense of mission to change user's life or living world. These types of fun can be applied to gamification when used in specific problem-solving tasks. But, serious fun requests a strong mission in a task, so the serious fun is not considered in this study.

Elements of gamification include the following [7].

- Score, defined as a level by ranking or a numerical record (often a total number of points) achieved in a game.
- Badge, defined as an emblem or distinguishing mark to indicate accomplishment.
- Leaderboard, which is a list ordered by real-time scores.
- Virtual currency, which is virtual money or money applicable only in an online setting, used to purchase goods and services.
- Gift, defined as an item of exchange such as a reward or coupon.
- Challenge, defined as a contest between users.

In this study, these elements are introduced to problem-solving tasks such as brainstorming in conjunction with the three categories of fun (easy, hard, and people fun).

3   Design of an Electronic Brainstorming System

We implemented an electronic brainstorming system using the blog software WordPress [10]. The interface screen of the brainstorming system is displayed in Figure 1. Descriptions of the gamification elements based on the three categories of fun are listed in Table 1. When using the system, a user can input an idea on the input area of the interface (Area 2 in Figure 1) and display it on a shared board. In addition, a user can add an idea to an existing idea by clicking on an adding mark (Area 3 in Figure 1). A user receives 10 points whenever he or she inputs an idea. If a user adds to an existing idea, both the user and author of the original idea each receive 10 points.

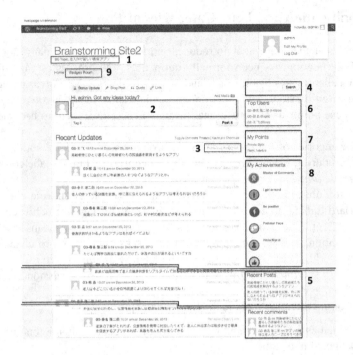

Fig. 1. Interface screen of the electronic brainstorming system with the following gamification elements indicated: Area 1, brainstorming theme; Area 2, input idea; Area 3, reply to an existing idea; Area 4, text-search function; Area 5, current ideas; Area 6, leaderboard; Area 7, user level and score; Area 8, badge list; Area 9, information about all badges

Table 1. Gamification elements in electronic brainstorming

Element	Main fun	Description
Level up	Hard fun	The goal is to attain an upper level of achievement.
Score	Easy fun	Involves easy user participation in brainstorming activities by simply obtaining a score.
Badge	Hard, Easy, People fun	Many types of badges support various kinds of achievements in hard, easy, and cooperative activities.
Leaderboard	People fun	People compete against one another for high scores.
Challenge	People fun	People attend earnestly brainstorming sessions with the goal of obtaining gifts.

A gamification feature entitled "level up" supports the category of *hard fun* by attaining an upper level of achievement, and the feature "score" supports *easy fun* by simply obtaining a score. These elements are shown in Area 7 in Figure 1.

The badge function provides 10 types of badges and can be used to support various types of fun. Conditions for attaining specific badges can be preset. Examples of badges include the following. A badge called "Hello World" supports the category of easy fun and can be obtained by a user inputting a single idea. A badge labeled "I get around" supports the category of hard fun and requires that a user add four ideas (i.e., four separate entries) to an existing idea. A badge called "Steady Worker," which also supports the category of hard fun, can be obtained when a user inputs 10 original ideas and adds three to an existing idea. Obtained badges are displayed in Area 8 in Figure 1.

The leaderboard supports the category of people fun and is displayed in Area 6 in Figure 1 ("top users"). Users can see other user ideas in Area 5. Although gift for a "Challenge" can be a virtual object that supports the category of people fun, our system does not support virtual money. To compensate for this deficiency, a physical gift could be used in support of this function.

4   Laboratory Experiments

Laboratory experiments were conducted to evaluate the brainstorming system using gamification. Participants in the experiments were 24 graduate students who were randomly assigned to eight groups of three persons each. The following two themes were used: "Theme 1: new smartphone application for children" and "Theme 2: new smartphone application for elderly people."

The following section describes procedures used in the study's experiments and evaluation methods employed.

4.1   Procedures

To evaluate the effectiveness of gamification used in a brainstorming system, four groups of 12 persons each met twice for 30-minute brainstorming sessions. The two sessions attended by each group were based on the two conditions; brainstorming is conducted either with gamification or without gamification. When a user in a gamification experiment obtained a high score, he or she received a gift or, in this experimental case, a system note. These participants were thus included in a competitive group.

To evaluate the effectiveness of cooperative gamification, four groups of 12 persons each participated in a single brainstorming session. In this experiment, when a group obtained a high score, all participants within the group received a gift. These participants were thus included in a cooperative group.

After a brainstorming session, participants completed a questionnaire that used a five-point scale. The questions were worded as follows. "Q1. Is the system easy to use?," "Q2. Are you interested in the session theme?," "Q3. Did you state your idea?," "Q4. Did the ideas of other participants affect your own idea?," "Q5. Was your curiosity stimulated?," "Q6. Did you feel like you were achieving your goal?," "Q7. Did you concentrate during the brainstorming session?," "Q8. Did you enjoy brainstorming with other participants?," "Q9. Did you feel competent when working with other participants?," and "Q10. Did you enjoy brainstorming in conjunction with the system?"

4.2   Evaluation Methods

Ideas generated from the brainstorming sessions were evaluated based on four criteria: number of ideas, fluency, flexibility, and originality. The number of ideas provided by each person was counted. The last three criteria were used based on [11]. Three researchers who did not participate in the experiments were asked to evaluate the ideas.

The fluency of ideas was defined as the ease at which participants provided reasonable and thoughtful ideas about the themes described previously (see the beginning of this section). If two of three evaluators judged an idea to be redundant or unrelated to the theme, the idea was not counted.

The flexibility of ideas was evaluated based on the diversity of participant viewpoints. Following the experiments, researchers produced a list of viewpoints (education, entertainment, game, health, music, social network, sport, trip, safety, and life style). Each idea was assigned to a viewpoint on the list. The number of assigned viewpoints was counted as the flexibility of ideas.

The originality of ideas was evaluated based on their uniqueness. If ideas of multiple participants were determined to be identical or similar, these ideas were not counted.

5   Results and Discussion

Because the sample size included fewer than 30 participants, the normal distribution of the number of ideas was validated by means of an F-test and their normal distribution was assumed. The two-tailed T-test was then used to statistically compare the number of ideas, fluency, flexibility, and originality. The number of ideas generated from the brainstorming sessions on Theme 1 was not significantly different from that generated from the brainstorming sessions on Theme 2.

However, the results from those groups that participated in two brainstorming sessions revealed that the second session affected the number of ideas significantly. Therefore, the data derived from the first brainstorming session that employed gamification was used to compare with the cooperative group.

5.1   Effects of Gamification

Table 2 shows the results of comparisons between those sessions that employed gamification and those that did not. In general, it reveals that the elements of gamification significantly improved the quality of ideas in terms of fluency, flexibility, and originality. Table 3 displays the results of the questionnaire about the effects of gamification. Comparison analysis revealed no significant differences.

The quality of ideas when gamification was used improved, but the results from the questionnaire indicated no significant difference. Numerical results of all answers to Questions 1 and 9 concerning gamification were higher than the neutral score. Thus, participants revealed that the system is easy to use when in a competitive setting and may promote a high quality of ideas. In addition, participants involved in gamification received badges for hard fun. These results indicate that individual ideas, when produced in conjunction with other participant ideas, may lead to idea fluency, originality, and flexibility.

Table 2. Effects of gamification based on the four criteria of idea quality

Four criteria	With gamification	Without gamification
Number of ideas	14.2	11.7
Fluency	12.8*	9.8
Flexibility	5.3*	4.1
Originality	7.9*	5.3

Two-tailed T-test: *$P < 0.05$, **$P < 0.01$

Table 3. Results of the questionnaire related to the effects of gamification

Questionnaire item	With gamification					Without gamification				
	1	2	3	4	5	1	2	3	4	5
Q1. Is the system easy to use?	0	0	0	7	5	0	1	0	5	6
Q2. Are you interested in the session theme?	0	1	2	7	2	0	0	1	8	3
Q3. Did you state your idea?	0	0	1	6	5	0	0	0	8	4
Q4. Did other participants' idea affect your idea?	0	2	4	6	0	1	3	2	6	0
Q5. Was your curiosity stimulated?	0	1	0	9	2	0	0	1	8	3
Q6. Did you feel like you were achieving your goal?	1	0	2	7	2	0	0	1	9	2
Q7. Did you concentrate during the brainstorming session?	0	1	1	8	2	0	0	1	6	5
Q8. Did you enjoy brainstorming with other participants?	0	1	1	8	2	0	1	0	9	2
Q9. Did you feel competence with other participants?	0	0	0	9	3	0	2	1	8	1
Q10. Did you enjoy brainstorming with the system?	0	1	0	8	3	0	0	0	8	4

Mann-Whitney U-test: *$P < 0.05$, **$P < 0.01$

5.2   Effects of Group Cooperation

Table 4 shows the results of comparisons between the cooperative and competitive groups. The results revealed no significant differences between the two groups. Table 5 shows the results of the questionnaire concerning the effects of group cooperation. The results revealed no significant differences.

It is assumed that performance expectations of the cooperative group may improve collaboration and lead to a group becoming more creative, but the laboratory experiments did not corroborate such assumptions about performance. Nevertheless, people fun is considered a key factor in organizational learning [7]. Therefore, the potential positive effects of group cooperation with gamification should be considered in the context of long-term system usage.

Table 4. Effects of cooperation based on the four criteria of idea quality

Four criteria	Cooperation	Competition
Number of ideas	16.5	15.3
Fluency	13.8	13.7
Flexibility	5.4	4.7
Originality	8.3	8.3

Two-tailed T-test: $*P < 0.05$, $**P < 0.01$

Table 5. Results of the questionnaire about the effects of cooperation

Questionnaire item	Cooperation					Competition				
	1	2	3	4	5	1	2	3	4	5
Q1. Is the system easy to use?	1	1	2	5	3	0	0	0	5	1
Q2. Are you interested in the session theme?	0	0	2	8	2	0	1	1	3	1
Q3. Did you state your idea?	0	1	0	8	3	0	0	1	3	2
Q4. Did other participants' idea affect your idea?	0	2	1	9	0	0	1	3	2	0
Q5. Was your curiosity stimulated?	0	1	2	8	1	0	0	0	4	2
Q6. Did you feel like you were achieving your goal?	1	1	3	6	1	1	0	1	4	0
Q7. Did you concentrate during the brainstorming session?	0	0	0	9	3	0	0	1	4	1
Q8. Did you enjoy brainstorming with other participants?	0	0	1	7	4	0	0	0	5	1
Q9. Did you feel competence with other participants?	0	1	2	7	2	0	0	0	4	2
Q10. Did you enjoy brainstorming with the system?	0	0	2	9	1	0	0	0	6	0

Mann-Whitney U-test: $*P < 0.05$, $**P < 0.01$

6   Concluding Remarks

This paper describes a brainstorming system that employs gamification elements. Three categories of fun were introduced into the system by using blog software. For this study, the elements of gamification are identified as: level up for hard fun, score for easy fun, leaderboard for people fun, gift for people fun, and badge for many forms of fun.

The laboratory experiments involved 24 participants and were conducted to investigate the effects of gamification on brainstorming. Brainstorming sessions both with and without gamification were administered. The results showed that gamification improved the quality of generated ideas in terms of fluency, flexibility, and originality, and revealed significant differences in results when compared to those from sessions that did not use gamification. In the gamification environment, no significant differences were found between cooperative and competitive groups. In addition, the effect of each category of fun was inconclusive based on questionnaire results.

In the future, we will develop network community and implement a long-term gamification system to promote brainstorming.

Acknowledgement. This research was partially supported by the Japan Society for the Promotion of Science (JSPS) and the Grant-in-Aid for Scientific Research (C) 24500143, 2014.

References

1. Osborn, A.F.: Applied Imagination, Revised edition. Charles Scribner's Sons (1957)
2. Dunnette, M.D., Campbell, J., Jaastad, K.: The Effect of Group Participation on Brain storming Effectiveness for Two Industrial Samples. Journal of Applied Psychology 47, 30–37 (1963)
3. Hymes, C.H., Olson, G.M.: Unblocking Brainstorming Through the Use of a Simple Group Editor. In: Proc. CSCW 1992, pp. 99–106. ACM Press (1992)
4. Wilson, C.: Brainstorming and Beyond. Morgan Kaufmann (2013)
5. Kelley, T.: The Art of Innovation. Crown Business (2001)
6. Zichermann, G., Gunningham, C.: Gamification by Design. O'Reilly (2011)
7. Hagel III, J., Brown, J.S., Davison, L.: The Power of Pull. Basic Books (2010)
8. Lazzaro, N.: Why We Play Games: Keys to More Emotion Without Story, http://xeodesign.com/xeodesign_whyweplaygames.pdf (accessed on April 21, 2014)
9. XEODSIGN: The 4 Keys to Fun, http://www.xeodesign.com/research.html (accessed on April 21, 2014)
10. WordPress, http://wordpress.org (accessed on April 4, 2014)
11. Furukawa, H., Yuizono, T., Kunifuji, S.: Idea Planter: A Backchannel Function for Foster-ing Ideas in a Distributed Brainstorming Support System. In: Proc. of KICSS 2013, pp. 92–103 (2013)

Difference between Standing and Seated Conversation over Meal toward Better Communication Support

Yasuhito Noguchi[1] and Tomoo Inoue[2]

[1] Graduate School of Library, Information and Media Studies,
University of Tsukuba, 1-2, Kasuga, Tsukuba, Ibaraki, 305-8550, Japan
noguchi@slis.tsukuba.ac.jp
[2] Faculty of Library, Information and Media Science,
University of Tsukuba, 1-2, Kasuga, Tsukuba, Ibaraki, 305-8550, Japan
inoue@slis.tsukuba.ac.jp

Abstract. It is known that conversation over a meal is better than the one without it. We often have a banquet when we socialize. We have two styles for such co-dining social activity; standing and seated. However we do not know if these styles matter for conversation. Therefore we have conducted an experimental study to investigate their differences. Findings which can be useful for designing conversation support are that the standing style 1) increases the number of utterances, nods and laughs, 2) makes a single utterance shorter, which helps crisp and vibrant conversation as a result, 3) increases turning to the speaker by the trunk, and 4) increases synchrony of eating behavior and makes eating slower.

Keywords: co-dining conversation, posture, standing conversation, seated conversation.

1 Introduction

A meal is indispensable to us. A meal not only has the role of nutrient intake but also serves a function to communicate with the partner. It is known that conversation over a meal is better than one without it. There is much research about "co-dining" [1].

We have two styles for such co-dining social activity; standing and seated. Although a participant can move only the upper half of the body in the seated style, they can move the whole body in the standing style. However, we do not know what influences the differences of these styles in co-dining. Therefore, we have conducted an experimental study to investigate their differences.

In the next section, related work is mentioned. In Section 3, details of the experiment are described. In Section 4, the analysis method and the results are presented, and Section 5 examines these results. The conclusion is given in Section 6.

T. Yuizono et al. (Eds.): CollabTech 2014, CCIS 460, pp. 62–76, 2014.

2   Related Work

2.1   Influence of Posture in Conversation

There is a large amount of research about influence of the posture in conversation. Bull et al. have conducted an experimental study to investigate the relation between posture and utterance styles in a two person conversation scenario [2]. Thomas et al. have described that participants in conversation raise the face when asking a question, and turn the head to their partner [3].They also have described that the participants keep the head away from their partner when answering the question. Argyle has summarized some research findings and mentioned the affective feature corresponding to the posture of an arm, a leg, and the body [4].

A posture is one of the nonverbal actions which conveys the inside of a speaker and a hearer unconsciously, and has relation with the utterance in conversation. In this research, these postures are not treated but we treat the difference of the standing style and the seated style.There is research which clarifies the feature of conversation in standing posture style, and in seated posture style. On the other hand, there is little research which compares the difference arising from these postures. Williams has reported the trend indicating that standing interpersonal distance provides a more sensitive measure of interpersonal distancing behavior than seated interpersonal distance [5]. However we do not know if these styles matter for conversation.

2.2   Co-dining

Recently, the research in co-dining has been approached. As the basic research of effective support in remote co-dining conversation, Furukawa et al. have compared a remote one and a face-to-face one. Furthermore, they have compared conversation showing the meal and not showing the meal in video-mediated table talk [6]. On the other hand, Inoue et al. have revealed that conversational behavior, including utterance and gesture, was more balanced among the participants in the meal condition [7]. Mukawa et al. have analyzed controlling hand-mouth-motions to the coexistence of conversation and a meal [8]. Although these studies have investigated co-dining in the seated style, we do not know whether these results are the same in the standing style. Therefore, we have conducted an experimental study to investigate their differences.

3   Experiment

3.1   Experiment Purpose

The purpose of an experiment is to clarify the difference of conversation in co-dining between the standing and seated style. Although a participant in the seated style is supported by a chair, he is also fixed at the chair's position. The chair supports him and fixes him simultaneously. Therefore, the standing style makes a participant's bodily motion more flexible than the seated style does. It is possible that such an environmental difference affects utterance action and eating behavior. This experiment compares the standing condition and the seated condition in the first meeting of a multi-party. "Standing condition" means that the participants are standing in co-dining. "Seated condition" means that the participants are seating in co-dining.

3.2   Experiment Participants

The participants in this experiment were made up of 1 set of 3 persons who are relations of the first time to meet each other in order to eliminate the influence by the difference in friends' degree of intimacy. Participants in this experiment are a total of 6 sets of 18 persons (12 male, 6 female, 22.6 years old of average age). Control, in particular by sex, was not performed. Each participant participated in both conditions. The number of the participants who were at a standing style meal previously, and the number of the participants who were at a seated style meal previously were equal. Moreover, a requirement of participating was that all participants should be in a "slightly hungry" state.

3.3   Experimental Setup

The experiment was conducted in the environment as shown in Fig. 1. A participant can move freely in a space which is of sufficient width to talk and eat. A table which is circular and 70 cm in diameter has been used. Regarding the height of the table, 70 cm has been adopted at the standing condition, and 90 cm has been adopted at the seated condition. At standing conditions, the height of the table was adjusted by placing a stand (made from plastic, height is 20 cm) under the table used at seated conditions. Generally, the height of the table used for a meal shall be 60 cm - 100 cm [9]. Because the tables for a standing condition currently sold are 80 cm - 100 cm, we had adopted 90 cm which is a mean value. On both conditions, as the circular table was surrounded, a participant's initial position has been arranged 120 degrees at intervals. Furthermore, the distance from the center of a table to the center of each participant's trunk was 70 cm. As a result, the distance of the initial position between each participant is set to about 120 cm and is a distance observed by a buffet-style party [10].

3.4   Meal

We used only one kind of snack as the meal in order to eliminate the influence by the kind of snacks. The snacks were piled on a white plate 20 cm in diameter at the center of the table. The drink was not given to the participants during the experiment, in order to eliminate influence. However, green tea was given to the participant who wanted it before the experiment started.

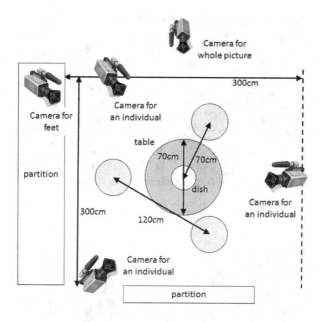

Fig. 1. Experimental setup

3.5   Experiment Procedure

The participant participated in both conditions on the same day. A break time of 10 minutes was taken between each condition. The experimenter told the participant the following six instructions. 1) The participant needs to participate in the session of conversation and a meal a total of 2 times. 2) Each session is filmed by video. 3) One session continues for 10 minutes. 4) After an experimenter has left, a participant can start a session at the participant's favorite timing. 5) A participant can move freely after a session starts. 6) A participant replies to the questionnaire and an interview after the end of a session. Before the session started, the experimenter gave green tea according to how thirsty a participant was, prepared the meal, and started the photography. After the experiment of each condition, a questionnaire investigation about the condition was conducted. The questionnaire investigation was of a free description type and the interview which compared both conditions was conducted after the end of an experiment of both conditions.

3.6   Acquisition of Data

A participant's action was recorded using the video camera. Three cameras have been set up in order to photograph the participants' upper half of the body. We have set these cameras in front of each participant for judging the existence of utterance and the direction of the face. One camera has been set at a distance

Fig. 2. A standing conversation scene

Fig. 3. A seated conversation scene

from participants in order to photograph the whole experimental setup. We have set this camera in order not to overlook a change of direction of a face or a trunk. Furthermore, we have also set one camera for photographing participants' feet in order to judge their trunk clearly. Cameras for an individual were taken with 1280 px × 720 px and 30 fps. Camera for whole picture and camera for feet were taken with 1920 px × 1080 px and 24 fps. A standing conversation scene is shown in Fig. 2, and a seated conversation scene is shown in Fig. 3. These figures have been photographed using the camera for the whole picture.

4   Analysis Method and Results

4.1   Video Analysis Method

We have analyzed the video, the answer to the questionnaire, and the interview in the experiment. The video of a total of 120 minutes (for 10 minutes after utterance of the beginning of 6 sets of both conditions) has been analyzed.

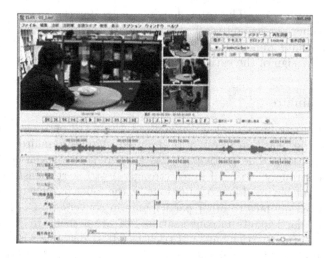

Fig. 4. Video analysis by ELAN

We have analyzed video using a video analysis tool, "ELAN" [11]. The video analysis scene is shown in Fig. 4. Labeling has been performed by two experimenters. First, two experimenters have carried out the labeling on the same video of 12 minutes, respectively. As a result, the coincidence rate (kappa coefficient) between experimenters was 1) 87.6%(k=0.74) in utterance, 2) 82.1% (k=0.69) in direction of a face, 3) 77.8% (k=0.64) in direction of a trunk, 4) 100% (k=1.00) in eating behavior. Since each kappa coefficient was 0.6 or more, and the degree of coincidence of the label between experimenters was high enough, two experimenters have shared the labeling of 90 percent which remained.

The TCU (Turn Construction Unit) was adopted as the labeling of utterance. Authorization of the boundary of a paragraph unit based on "Corpus of Spontaneous Japanese" [12] [13]. Labeling was performed for from the time of onset of one paragraph to termination time as one TCU. The utterance from which the right of utterance was acquired was "the usual utterance". Moreover, "nods" and "laughter" were counted. The portion without all participants' utterance was counted as "silence."

In stand-up meal conditions and seating conditions, the flexibility of the body has a difference and a difference may arise in the frequency and rate which turn a face and a trunk to a speaker. Therefore, direction of a participant's face and a trunk was analyzed. The center of the body containing a chest and an abdomen is defined as a trunk.

The period after putting snack confectionery into a mouth, until it is swallowed, was defined as the eating behavior and was counted. Moreover, the synchronous situation of the eating behavior was also observed. After another participant lifted his hand from the plate, the action of reaching for the snack within 0.89 second was counted, such as the eating behavior synchronized. 0.89 second is the average delay time concerning the reaction and operation in the case of conversation [14]. The eater does not reach for the snack with hesitation while another participant reaches for the plate. Therefore, the action which reaches for the plate immediately after the other participant takes the snack can be judged as the sign of the eating behavior being synchronized.

4.2   Questionnaire

In the questionnaire investigation, the data of 4 sets (12 persons: 9 male, 3 female), except the defective result, was analyzed. A questionnaire consists of a total of 40 questions. The participant has answered with seven choices (from "1: I disagree strongly" to "7: I agree strongly") of Likert measures. In order to measure about having done so intentionally, the following five questions were set up: "I turned my face to other participants in conversation"; "I turned my trunk to other participants in conversation"; "I ate a snack frequently to the same timing as other participants"; "I tried to adjust distance with a partner"; "I tried to express my feeling using a gesture". In order to measure the intimacy of relations with friends, the following seven questions were set up [15], "I was able to show my gentle feeling attitude"; "I was able to talk honestly"; "I was able to rely on the partner"; "The partner understood me"; "I got interested in a partner"; "We have similar hobbies"; "The partner got interested in me". In order to measure a communication participation style, the following nine questions were set up [16], "I talked with nodding"; "I tried to understand the partner's idea"; "I listened to a speaker's opinion"; "I did not interfere in conversation"; "I talked actively"; "I developed conversation"; "I did not make silence"; "I was able to get a partner to express an opinion"; "I asked without withholding". The following six questions were set up as subjective evaluation about conversation: "I talked happily"; "I talked cooperatively"; "It was easy to talk"; "I was deep in conversation"; "Conversation was valuable"; "Conversation was made with the affirmative attitude". The following seven questions were set up as subjective evaluation about a meal: "I enjoyed my snack"; "I tasted"; "I bit well"; "I ate slowly"; "I was deep in meal"; "I thought that I ate together with partners"; "It was easy to reach for a plate". The following six questions were set up as evaluation about the consciousness to other participants: "I felt intimacy for the partner"; "I would like to know the partners more"; "I was nervous when talking with the partners"; "I was frank with the partners"; "I thought that the partner was nervous"; "Time passed quickly".

Moreover, in order to remove the influence by an order of a questionnaire, the question paper with which an order of all the items was replaced at random was prepared for each participant. Also, the questionnaire of the free writing about comparison of both conditions was set up. Participants replied to the interview about the reason for having chosen their answer after the reply of free description.

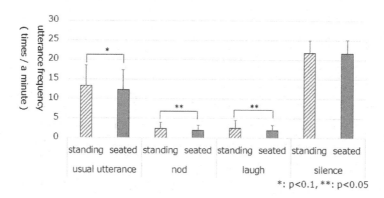

Fig. 5. Utterance frequency

4.3   Results of Video Analysis

The test used, common to the data described below, is described. The Shapiro-Wilk test was used about the normality of the data. The F-test was used for the difference of distribution of two data groups. Moreover, the error bar in the below-mentioned figure shows standard deviation in common.

Utterance. The results of frequencies of the usual utterance, nods, laughter, and silence (the times per a minute) are shown in Fig. 5. Because the results, except for silence, were normal distribution data, and the results' distributions have no differences, a student-t-test (one side) was performed about the difference of the results of both conditions. The results of the usual utterance were 13.3 times per a minute in the standing condition and 12.2 times per a minute in the seated condition. The standing condition tends to increase the number of utterances (t(17)=1.54, p=0.071). The results of nods were 2.4 times per a minute in the standing condition and 1.9 times per a minute in the seated condition. Similarly, the results of laugher were 2.5 times per a minute in the standing condition and 1.9 times per a minute in the seated condition. The standing condition increases the number of nods and laugher (nods: t(17)=2.35, p=0.015, laugher: t(17)=1.54, p=0.071). Because the results of silence were NOT normal distribution data, the Wilcoxon signed-rank test was performed about the difference of the results of both conditions. The results of silence were 21.8 times per minute in the standing condition and 21.7 times per a minute in the seated condition, and both did not have the difference (Z=-0.105, p=0.917).

The results of rates of each utterance actions are shown in Fig. 6. Because the results were normal distribution data, and the results' distributions have no differences, a student-t-test (one side) was performed about the difference of the results of both conditions. The results of the usual utterance were 24.8% in the standing condition and 23.9% in the seated condition, and both did not have a difference (t(17)=0.522, p=0.304). The results of nods were 2.7% in the standing condition and 2.3% in the seated condition. Similarly the results of

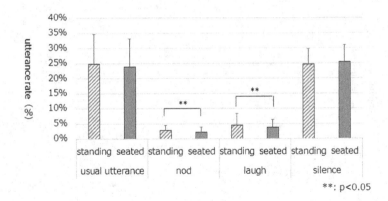

Fig. 6. Utterance rate

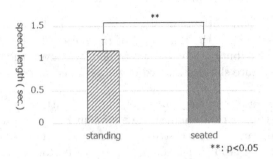

Fig. 7. Speech length

laugher were 4.5% in standing condition and 3.7% in seated condition. The standing condition increases the rates of nods and laugher (nods: $t(17)=2.02$, $p=0.030$, laugher: $t(17)=1.81$, $p=0.044$). The results of silence were 24.7% in the standing condition and 25.4% in the seated condition, and both did not have the difference ($t(5)=-0.327$, $p=0.378$).

The results of speech length are shown in Fig. 7. Because the result was normal distribution data, and the result's distribution have no differences, student-t-test (one side) was performed about the difference of the results of both conditions. The results of the speech length were 1.11 seconds in the standing condition and 1.18 seconds in the seated condition. The standing condition decreases the speech length ($t(17)=-1.76$, $p=0.048$).

Face and Trunk Directions. The results of face and trunk directions to the speaker in frequency and rates are shown in Fig. 8.

Because the results of face direction were normal distribution data, and the result's distribution have no differences, student-t-test (one side) was performed about the difference of the results of both conditions. The results of the face directions in frequency were 13.6 times per a minute in the standing condition

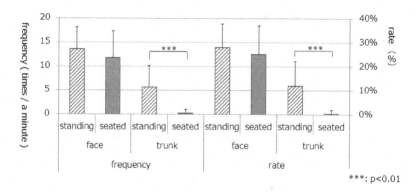

Fig. 8. Face and trunk directions to the speaker in frequency and rates

and 11.9 times per a minute in the seated condition, both did not have the difference (t(17)=1.16, p=0.131). Similarly the results of the face direction in rate were 28.1% in the standing condition and 25.2% in the seated condition, both did not have the difference (t(17)=0.905, p=0.189)

Because the results of trunk direction were NOT normal distribution data, the Wilcoxon signed-rank test was performed about the difference of the results of both conditions. The results of the trunk directions in frequency were 5.7 times per a minute in standing condition and 0.3 times per a minute in seated condition. The result of the trunk directions in frequency in the standing condition was higher than the result in the seated condition (t(17)=-3.62, p=0.0003). Similarly the results of the trunk directions in rate were 12.0% in the standing condition and 0.5% in the seated condition. The result in rate in the standing condition was higher than the result in the seated condition (t(17)=-3.62, p=0.0003). However, chairs' foot used in seated condition were fixed style. It might have not been easy to change orientation of participant's trunk compared to using turn-style chairs.

Eating Behavior. The results of eating frequency and rate are shown in Fig. 9. Because the results of eating behavior were normal distribution data, and the result's distribution has not difference, a student-t-test (one side) was performed about the difference of the results of both conditions. The results of eating frequency were 0.79 times per minute in the standing condition and 0.68 times per a minute in the seated condition, both did not have the difference (t(17)=0.847, p=0.204). Because the result of eating rate was NOT normal distribution data, the Wilcoxon signed-rank test was performed about the difference of the results of both conditions. The results of the eating rate were 13.9% in the standing condition and 11.6% in the seated condition. The result in rate in standing condition tends to increase the eating rate (Z=-1.67, p=0.094).

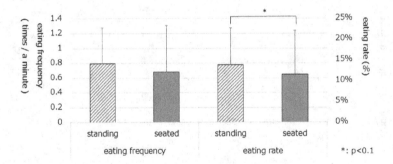

Fig. 9. Eating frequency and rate

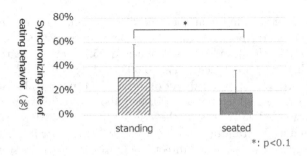

Fig. 10. Synchronizing rate of eating behavior

The results of synchronizing rate of eating behavior are shown in Fig. 10. Because the results of synchronizing rate of eating behavior were NOT normal distribution data, the Wilcoxon signed-rank test was performed about the difference of the results of both conditions. The results of the eating rate were 30.6% in the standing condition and 17.9% in the seated condition. The result in rate in the standing condition tends to increase the synchronizing rate of eating behavior (Z=-1.85, p=0.065).

4.4   Questionnaire Results

The Wilcoxon signed-rank test was performed about the difference of the results of both conditions. The results of the questionnaire with a significant difference and a significant tendency are shown in Table 1.

In the results in the questionnaire for conversation, the score of "I turned my face to other participants in conversation" in the standing condition was lower than the score in the seated condition. On the contrary, the scores of "I tried to adjust distance with partners", "I talked happily", and "I was nervous when talking with the.partners" in the standing condition were higher than the scores in the seated condition. In the results in the questionnaire for the meal,

Table 1. Questionnaire results

Questions	Average score in standing condition	Average score in seated condition	Wilcoxon signed-rank test p value
【Questionnaire for conversation】			
I turned my face to other participants	6.25	6.58	**0.046
I tried to adjust distance with a partner	4.17	3.08	**0.012
I talked happily	6.08	5.50	**0.034
I was nervous by talking with the partners	4.08	3.33	**0.024
【Questionnaire for meal】			
I ate a snack frequently to the same timing	5.58	3.42	**0.015
I thought that I ate together with partners	4.67	3.42	*0.059
I enjoyed my snack	5.08	3.92	*0.078

** $p < 0.05$, * $p < 0.1$

the score of "I ate a snack frequently to the same timing as other participants" in the standing condition was higher than the score in the seated condition. The scores of "I thought that I ate together with partners" and "I enjoyed my snack" in the standing condition tend to be higher than the scores in the seated condition. There was no difference in the other questionnaire.

Next, the answers by free description are described. There was opinion about conversation that "It is much easier to make a gesture in the standing condition than in the seated condition". On the contrary, there were opinions that "I felt relaxed to talk and talked calmly in the seated condition". There was opinion about the meal that "It is much easier to reach for a snack in the standing condition than in the seated condition". On the other hand, the opinion "I was able to eat calmly" was seen in the seated conditions.

5 Discussion

5.1 Utterance

It was revealed that the standing condition increases the frequency of utterances, and increases the frequency and rate of nods and laughs from Fig. 5 and Fig. 6. Although it is known that a speaker's amount of utterance will increase by the effect of a hearer's nod [17], the increase of the utterance action as sympathy, such as nod and laugh, and the increased tendency of utterance frequency have also been simultaneously observed in this experiment. Moreover, Fig. 7 showed that the standing conditions of speech length were shorter than in seated conditions. In other words, it is shown that standing style makes single utterance shorter, which helps crisp and vibrant conversation.

On the other hand, in free description, opinions that "I felt relaxed to talk and talked calmly in the seated condition" were seen in seated conditions. This shows a possibility that the posture of conversation can be used according to intention and the purpose of conversation. It is considered that changing meal style is a kind of conversation support method although changing posture is not a technical solution. If the conference room which changes the form of a seat according to the kind and phase of a meeting is developed, we surmise that it is effective.

In addition, although the meal style was used in this experiment, there is room for examination about whether the same findings are acquired in conversation without a meal.

5.2   Face and Trunk Directions

It was revealed that the standing condition increases the frequency and rate of turning trunk to speaker from Fig. 8. An action of turning trunk to speaker is posture of listening actively. It could be easy to recognize the other participant as listener for speaker in standing style. On the other hand, conforming the direction of trunk has a beneficent influence in carrying information [18]. Co-dining in standing style is considered as better for conversation because it conveys richer body orientation.

Although both conditions did not have the difference in frequency and in rate of turning the face to the speaker from Fig. 8, the score of "I turned my face to other participants in conversation" in the standing condition was lower than the score in the seated condition from table 1. In addition, there were no differences of both conditions about the questionnaire that "I turned my trunk to other participants in conversation". These results show that a participant's subjective opinion and actual action have not necessarily agreed about the direction of a face or a trunk. Furukawa has revealed that because eating behavior is a daily action, the participants are not conscious of their gaze [6]. Similarly, since to change direction of a face and a trunk in the standing style is a natural act, it is considered that participants are not conscious of turning their face and trunk.

5.3   Eating Behavior

It was revealed that the standing condition increases synchrony of eating behavior from Fig. 10. In addition, a standing condition give the participants the impression of "I ate a snack frequently to the same timing as other participants", "I thought that I ate together with partners", "I enjoyed my snack" from Table 1. It is shown that the contents of co-dining may change although the difference among both of the co-dining style is only a participant's posture.

From Fig. 9, it turned out that the eating rate in the standing condition has a tendency to be higher than the one in the seated condition. However, there was no difference of eating frequency between both conditions. In other words, participants in standing style have eaten slowly. The synchronization of eating behavior takes place in the scene of co-dining, and influencing the amount of meals is known [19]. Furthermore, when a participant has a meal together with an interface agent, it is shown that the time of eating is prolonged compared with the case that there is no meal of an interface agent [20]. Similarly, the increases of the synchronizing rate of eating behavior and the time of eating have also been simultaneously observed in this experiment. Eating slowly is treated as important in health guidance [21]. Co-dining in standing style is considered as better in health-care because it makes the participants eat slowly.

6 Conclusion

In this paper, we have conducted an experimental study to investigate differences of standing style and seated style in co-dining of a multi-party. From the results, findings which can be useful for designing conversation support are that the standing style 1) increases the number of utterances, nods and laughs, 2) makes single utterance shorter, which helps crisp and vibrant conversation as a result, 3) increases turning to the speaker by the trunk, and 4) increases synchrony of eating behavior and makes eating slower. It was revealed that a participant's posture influences co-dining conversation, and that standing style increases the effect of co-dining.

References

1. Toyama, N.: Acquirement of the concept of the "Dining": Examining changes from elementary school children to college students through a questionnaire. Journal of Home Economics of Japan 41(8), 707–714 (1990)
2. Bull, P., Brown, R.: The role of postural change in dyadic conversation. British Journal of Social and Clinical Psychology 16(1), 29–33 (1977)
3. Thomas, A., Bull, P.: The role of pre-speech posture change in dyadic interaction. British Journal of Social Psychology 20(2), 105–111 (1981)
4. Argyle, M.: Bodily communication, 2nd edn. Methuen & Co. Ltd., London (1988)
5. Williams, J.: Personal space and its relation to extraversion introversion. Canadian Journal of Behavioural Science/Revue Canadienne des Sciences du Comportement 3(2), 156–160 (1971)
6. Furukawa, D., Inoue, T.: Showing meal in video-mediated table talk makes conversation close to face-to-face. IPSJ Journal 54(1), 266–274 (2013)
7. Inoue, T., Otake, M.: Effect of meal in triadic table talk: Equalization of speech and gesture between participants. The Transaction of Human Interface Society 13(3), 19–29 (2011)
8. Mukawa, N., Tokunaga, H., Yuasa, M., Tsuda, Y., Tateyama, K., Kasamatsu, C.: Analysis on utterance behaviors embedded in eating actions: How are conversations and hand-mouth-motions controlled in three-party table talk? The Transactions of the Institute of Electronics, Information and Communication Engineers J94-A(7), 500–508 (2011)
9. Japan Interior Architescts/Designers' Association. Table design. RIKUYOSHA Co., Ltd., Tokyo (2006)
10. Hall, E.: The Hidden Dimension. Doubleday, New York (1966)
11. Max Planck Institute for Psycholinguistics, ELAN, The Language Archive, http://www.lat-mpi.eu/tools/elan (Refer March 28, 2014)
12. Maruyama, T., Takanashi, K., Uchimoto, K.: Corpus of Spontaneous Japanese. National Institute for Japanese Language and Linguistics, Report 124, 255–322 (2006)

13. Enomoto, M., Ishizaki, M., Koiso, H., Den, Y., Mizukami, E., Yano, H.: A statistical investigation of basic units for spoken interaction analysis 104(445), 45–50 (2004)
14. Kanda, T., Kamashima, M., Imai, M., Ono, T., Sakamoto, D., Ishiguro, H., Anzai, Y.: Embodied Cooperative behavior for a Humanoid Robot that Communicates with Humans. Journal of the Robotics Society of Japan 23(7), 898–909 (2005)
15. Yoshioka, K.: The Satisfaction in Peer Relationship in terms of Self-Acceptance and the Discrepancies between Ideal and Real Peer Relationship. The Japanese Journal of Adolescent Psychology 13, 13–30 (2002)
16. Fujimoto, M.: COMPASS indicates participants' communication participation styles. Japanese Journal of Social Psychology 23(3), 290–297 (2008)
17. Matarazzo, J., Saslow, G., Wien, A., Weitman, M., Allen, B.: Interviewer head nodding and interviewee speech duration. Psychotherapy Theory Research & Practice 1(2), 54–63 (1964)
18. Ono, T., Imai, M., Kanda, T., Ishiguro, H.: Embodied Communication Emergent from Mutual Physical Expression between Humans and Robots. IPSJ Journal 42(6), 1348–1358 (2001)
19. Conger, J., Conger, A., Costanzo, P., Wright, K., Matter, J.: The effect of social cues on the eating behavior of obese and normal subjects. J. Pers. 48(2), 258–271 (1980)
20. Shiohara, T., Inoue, T.: Influence of a co-dining agent on a user's dining. IPSJ SIG Technical Report, 2013-DCC-4(12), 1–8 (2013)
21. Kubota, O., et al.: Relationship between Lifestyle and Body Mass Index: Analyses of 6,826 Adults who Underwent Health Check-ups. Official Journal of Japan Society of Ningen Dock 25(4), 626–632 (2010)

Study of Face-to-Face Dyadic Conversation Behavior on Uneven Meal Distribution Setting for Designing an Attentive Listening Agent

Hiromi Hanawa and Tomoo Inoue

Graduate School of Library, Information and Media Studies, University of Tsukuba,
Kasuga1-2, Tsukuba, Ibaraki, 305-8550, Japan
{hanawa,inoue}@slis.tsukuba.ac.jp

Abstract. A conversation over a meal and its support as a research topic has been gaining attention. Although all the researches so far assumed all participants have a meal, this paper points out the uneven meal distribution setting as an additional case to analyze. After conducting a face-to-face dyadic conversation experiment, analyses show that uneven meal distribution induces the narrator-active listener structure in dyadic conversation at a table. Accordingly the setting elicits attentive listening communication and proposed design of attentive listening agents.

Keywords: Attentive Listening, Dyadic Interaction, Listening Agent, Conversation over meal, Communication Aid, Dialogue, Dining Table, Table Talk, Face-to-face.

1 Introduction

Having a meal is a familiar issue in our daily life, and a conversation across a table is quite common activity for people. Previous discourse analyses and study of communication aid tools contained little occasion when actors sit at a table and dine, recently a dyadic conversation and its assistance has been drawing attention as a specific research field.

Previously the scene of all attendees' discourse with having a meal was analyzed for this research topic regardless of the asymmetric meal distributing subject matter [1, 2, 3]. Some of the few exceptional researches focused on the way to alter the status from participants' incapable of dining to capable one or employing manipulative control to exercise the uniformed dyadic conversation [4, 5].

Above mentioned studies are unsatisfactory to consider daily conversational circumstances at dining tables, for example, a husband coming back home late at night sits at the table to talk with his wife serves dinner even though she had finished dinner earlier. Also the case is very common to meet someone at a restaurant to eat something and wait until the other comes, and the first comer subsequently finishes eating to talk ever since the last comer orders and starts eating. These cases should be analyzed as subsequent applied matters of the field, conversations over the unequally distributed meal are discussed as an additional case in this paper.

T. Yuizono et al. (Eds.): CollabTech 2014, CCIS 460, pp. 77–85, 2014.

This uneven setting at a table, that was one with a meal but the other, was not considered to organize an exploratory research, firstly the basic dyadic conversation was examined as a default setting, and then the unequal meal distribution setup with actors' discourse analyses made a comparison with other constraints.

Consequently experimental data supposes attentive listening is installed in the scene of the uneven meal setting between actors. This paper proposes an attentive listening agent after stating of an exploratory analysis.

2   Dyadic Interaction on Uneven Meal Distribution

For discourse analysis in a circumstance of the asymmetric meal setup, both of quantitative and qualitative analysis by questionnaire survey was conducted. It was compared to the data set of "Co-Dining" which was a basic setting of both actors had a conversation with a meal at the same time, and "Non-Dining" that neither of them took meals and had only a dyadic interaction in states of mutually facing at a table [10]. Uneven meal distribution setting made across a table is "Asymmetric-Dining" that is uniqueness of this paper and also it was examined especially to compare with other two explicit constraints.

2.1   Experiment

A experiment organized three settings to compare each constraints. Participants of experiments were 12 college students that had 4 pairs of male students and 2 pairs of female students. Each single pairs were friends and examined in three different constraints that were explained above, and the order of participation was randomly changed in each pairs to setoff order effects. The duration of its entire process to undergo three constraints is two days for each pairs, and the first half of all pairs had "Asymmetric-Dining" with meal for one and then had it without meal for the other side of pairs. The rest of all pairs had "Non-Dining" constraints firstly and next conducted "Co-Dining", these process took counterbalance at the end. Overall the definition in this paper, the basic setup both attendees enjoyed meals with a conversation is "Co-Dining", neither of actors had meals and exercised face-to-face interaction is "Non-Dining", and "Asymmetric-Dining" is the scene of only one side at a table was with a meal but the other was not to have a conversation.

Menu was curry and rice, tea, and spoon was provided to intake. To make it natural behavior, experiments were conducted only on lunch and dinnertime, and underwent for two days unless actors continued eating at a moment. In these two days for each pairs, on one day participants had "Asymmetric-Dining" and on the other day "Co-Dining" and "Non-Dining" had examined amongst all pairs.

Figure 1 is a model of installation of three scenes, it possesses the uniformed interpersonal distance setting as 120cm that is supposed to be a normal unit in friendly relationship. Conversational topics were firstly given and flexibly alternative depending on the context on each pairs. Time constraints toward each scene were almost

10 mins for "Co-Dining", "Non-Dining", and "Asymmetric-Dining" to count time shifting into consideration. Entire processes of experiments were recorded and all participants had questionnaire surveys after the set of experiments.

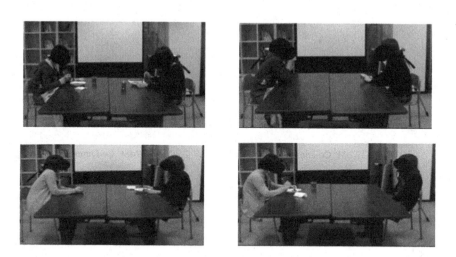

Fig. 1. This is an example of a figure caption. Figure captions are positioned below the figure.

2.2   Method of Analysis

2.2.1   Video Observation

Software of video observation is ELAN that analyzed 3 mins of each conditions or settings with constraints. It was recognized speech units that contained longer than 100ms Inter-Pausal Unit [11] after each speech utterances. In this paper ELAN tagged a "normal speech" in a conversation according to the context, that was categorized as "laughter", "silence", and "filler" that was vocalization of listening sounds [12].

2.2.2   Questionnaire Survey

Actors' subjective evaluations answered questionnaire sheets with a grade scaling method. Each 7 grades were 1=strongly disagree, 2=disagree, 3=relatively disagree, 4=neither agree nor disagree, 5=relatively agree, 6=agree, 7=strongly agree, nominal answers were calculated as total scores. The list of survey asked 28 question items about consciousness toward speech, sight, and a meal. The order of questions was randomly changed in every single pairs to cancel out a psychological effect.

2.3   Result

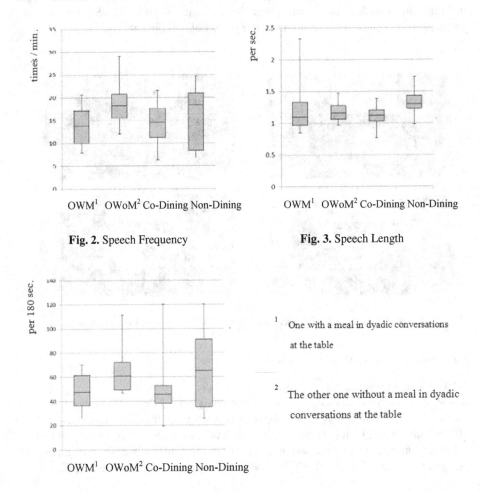

Fig. 2. Speech Frequency

Fig. 3. Speech Length

1 One with a meal in dyadic conversations at the table

2 The other one without a meal in dyadic conversations at the table

Fig. 4. Total Speech Length

2.3.1   Video Observation

Conversations under each constraint investigated a cumulative frequency of utterances, length of speech, and an entire length of series of vocalization. The "Asymmetric-Dining" constraint had two explicit unevenly distributed settings as one was with a meal but the other was not, here we defined each sides as "OWM" and "OWoM" to investigate separately.

Figure 2 shows a unit basis speech utterance frequency, Figure 3 is speech length per seconds, and Figure 4 is a cumulative sum of total speeches within 180 seconds. Those figures used mean, quartile, minimum and max of the statistical analysis. Figure 2 clarifies two things, firstly OWoM Speech Frequency is higher than OWM, it means the person who doesn't have a meal in dyadic conversation at a table speaks more frequently than the other one who have a meal. Secondly there are similarities between OWM and Co-Dining and also OWoM and Non-Dining in Speech Frequency, that is, the one without meal in an asymmetric meal setup is likely to be Non-Dining constraint's Speech Frequency, as well as the other one with meal is alike Co-Dining.

The data sets indicated that initial setoff speeches of "OWoM" were more frequent than "OWM", that was, the "OWoM" utterance frequency 18.2 times per min was beyond "OWM" 13.8 times per min according to Figure 2. There was not much difference in a speech length per second between "OWM" 1.1 seconds and "OWoM" 1.2 seconds about Figure 3. Figure 4 suggested that "OWoM" side's 60.8 sec had much more amount of speech utterances than its "OWM" side's 47.6 sec.

From all of these three figures in comparison of each cases, it is supposed to be likelihood of "Co-Dining" and "OWM" are in similarities and also "Non-Dining" and "OWoM", which results from the meal distribution disequilibrium.

From all above analyses that is currently insufficient of the statistical data sets, it is suggested that one sit at a table without a meal can become a potential main speaker in a conversation in which the scene of conditions is an unevenly distributed meal setting on a face-to-face dining table.

2.3.2 Questionnaire Survey

Table 1 is the outcome of the conducted survey. Each score is an average point of grading scale questionnaire survey. Comparing "OWM" with "OWoM" in question No.5, No.7, and No. 23, data sets show a little high score in OWoM. This means participants felt more agreeable with speech consciousness related question such as "I often speak up", "I tried not to keep quiet", and "I tried to avoid making silence". Since it was not also seen in comparison with Co-Dining and Non-Dining settings, It seems that one without a meal in dyadic conversation consciously became a leading speaker amongst the two to some extent. This results coincidentally matched the outcome of that "OWoM" in Figure 2 and 4 pointed out larger number than other three constraints in Speech Frequency and cumulative sum of total speeches. Accordingly the result was supported by both of quantitative and qualitative analyses, which is that one without a meal in dyadic conversation across a table consciously became a leading speaker among the two.

There is not statistical work in Table 1 since the amount of data set is not enough, It seems that the score of "OWM" in No.2 and No.6 are relatively large in question of "My words were too short" and "I tried to say something briefly", thus attendees spoke less while eating on Asymmetric-Dining. However Figure 3 actually represents there are not much difference in Total Speech Length among one with meal and the other one without meal at a table. This is not a main topic in this paper instead a unique results.

Remarkable point in OWM and OWoM are shown in No.10 and No.12 for the question of "I looked at my hands" and "I looked at peer's hands", that is both sides of Asymmetric-Dining table gazed at food.

Table 1. Questionnaire Score Result

(1=Strongly Disagree, 7=Strongly Agree, Total Score Average: N=12)

No	Question Items	OWM	OWoM	Co-Dining	Non-Dining
1	I often spoke with peer.	4.7	5.4	5.3	5.3
2	My words were too short.	4.5	3.6	3.3	3.0
3	Moment of silence was short period of time.	4.8	4.9	4.6	5.3
4	Speakers often took turns during talking.	4.6	4.6	4.4	4.6
5	I often speak up to my peer.	4.1	5.2	5.1	4.7
6	I tried to say something briefly.	3.5	2.8	2.5	2.7
7	I tried not to keep quiet.	3.9	4.8	5.0	4.5
8	I tried to take turns to talk.	4.3	3.4	4.6	4.0
9	Timing of starting talking often overlaps.	2.8	2.8	2.8	3.2
10	I often looked at my hands.	5.5	2.3	4.4	3.3
11	I often looked into my peer's face.	4.2	5.3	5.3	5.8
12	I often looked at my peer's hands	1.7	4.6	2.9	3.1
13	I pretty much enjoyed a conversation.	5.9	5.9	6.0	5.8
14	It was easy and confortable to talk.	5.3	5.3	5.3	4.8
15	I understood what my peer talked to me.	5.8	6.1	5.8	5.8
16	My peer understood what I talked about.	5.3	5.3	5.6	5.1
17	I enjoyed having a meal with a conversation.	5.5		5.8	
18	Having lunch/dinner was easy and relaxing.	5.2		5.2	
19	It was hard to talk to my peer due to a meal.		3.0		
20	I often looked into my peer's dining.		5.0		
21	I paid attention to my peer's meal progress.	3.8	4.1	3.9	
22	I didn't hesitate to speak up to my peer.	5.8	5.8	6.0	6.3
23	I tried to avoid making silence.	3.7	4.8	4.1	4.6
24	Having a conversation was like a pair work.	4.9	4.6	5.4	5.4
25	Atmosphere of a conversation was good.	5.8	5.7	5.4	5.3
26	I behave quite naturally.	5.6	5.1	5.8	4.8
27	Given conversational topics were good.	5.6	4.9	5.4	4.6
28	I was interested in a conversational topic.	5.8	5.4	6.0	5.3

No.13, No.14, No.15, No.16, and No.22, these all question answers have not much difference in OWM and OWoM and also found proximity with Co-Dining and Non-Dining constraints. These question items are "I pretty much enjoyed conversation.", "It was easy to talk to my peer.", "I understood what my peer talked to me.", "My peer understood what I talked about.", "I didn't hesitate to speak up." Therefore it can be said that Asymmetric-Dining allows usual mealtime communication and to have a conversation as Co-Dining and Non-Dining setting. No.19 "It was hard to talk to my peer while s/he took a meal." scored fairly low in OWoM also sustained this result. All experiments under three constraints shows that one without meal in dyadic conversation at a table often becomes a leading speaker, and the other side at a table with meal has a tendency to be a listener.

3   Attentive Listening Agent

3.1   Active Listening Communication

Experiments show that one side without dining in dyadic conversation at a table becomes a main speaker and the other dining side becomes a listener, which is uneven meal distribution induces the relationship of a narrator and an active listener. This is what dining activity causes at a table, which is this dining activity facilitates narrator-listener structure by its dining action. Experimental outcomes suppose that the OWoM side often makes a role of a narrator and OWM side positively hears it from an uneven meal distribution on a face-to-face dining table. Hence it realizes the attentive listening communication is to listen to talk rather to judge or talk back. In other word, It's possible to let someone else listen to you only if you have a person to dine. In the case of the married couple mentioned earlier, the husband listens to his wife during dinner, that is, the wife can talk as much as she wants and he seems to give a satisfactory amount of feed back without judging her. That is a wonderful application of communication that encourages and soothes interpersonal transaction by the chemistry of listening.

3.2   Proposal of a Listening Agent

Experimental analysis found that asymmetric meal distribution induces the relationship of a narrator and an active listener. Here we discuss the possibility to create relationship between narrator and listener by non-verbal behavior using the experimental outcome. Kobayashi et al. employed linguistic approach with basic listening sequence skills to implement active listening agents and design good listener skills, but concluded the speech recognition result included errors. [17] Additionally Watanabe et al. developed both verbal and nonverbal communication robot which activates human interaction on a basis of speech input, this robot motion as a listener responds at the timing equivalent to human nodding. [18] Previous researches stated that anthropomorphic agents and dialogue agents affect the human cognition and behaviors. The old dialogue agent ELIZA [13] was a counselor that users input texts to talk to her as its against a real human being, it was reasonable to personalize artificial goods and treat it as real human beings [14]. Most of artificial agents provided information and persuaded someone in the past, welfare service for elderly care now requires dialogue agents and it also needs active listening agents. Research for the listening agent has started yet its design is not made [15]. Dining activity is quite simple implication of activity, which is possible to prompt narrator-listener structure that is found by our face-to-face dining experiment. Richardson says "Active listening is a way of counseling that involves listening characterized by empathy, genuineness and warmth. It facilitates the clients understanding his/her own opinion and builds the clients' self-confidence." [19] In our listening agent deign proposal, simple but strong implementation is novel, which is agents' dining activity is physically feasible as a gestured language to facilitate human interaction.

This experiment provides the opportunity to see an uneven meal distribution states causing propensity for active listening. Thinking about the design of listening agents instead of dialogue agents, agent's dining activity can be feasible for one of the choices. Listening agents require means of hearing aptitudes that is adopted a gestured language now that it relatively makes less speech utterances. Paro [15] proposed pet animals for listening agents, humanoid listening agents could be in demand more in the future but unknown, this paper suggests one alternative choice.

4 Implications

This paper examined and reported the dyadic interactive communication with an uneven distributed meal setting at a table, the result indicated the table status can cause propensity for the attentive listening communication style. It also stated an applicable design of the listening agent will be required in the future, therefore to propose humanoid agents' design with dining activity at a table can be applicable. Experiments were only conducted using human being, it is also mentioned to see if dialogue agents and human at a table can pull out the same experimental results.

Acknowledgements. We would like to express our appreciation to Yuya Higaki who helped us to organize this experiment. This research was partially supported by the JSPS Grants-in-Aid for Scientific Research No. 23500158 and No. 26330218.

References

1. Mukawa, N.: Analysis and Application of Dining Communication: Development system to share enjoyment of eating. Journal of Information Processing Society of Japan 52(11), 1397–1402 (2011) (in Japanese)
2. Grimes, A., Harper, R.: Celebratory technology: New directions for food research in HCI. In: Proceedings of the ACM-CHI Conference on Human Factors in Computing Systems 2008, pp. 467–476 (2008)
3. Comber, R., Ganglbauer, E., Choi, J.H.-J., Hoonhout, J., Rogers, V., O'Hara, K., Maitland, J.: Food and interaction design: designing for food in everyday life. In: Proceedings of the 12th ACM-SIGCHI Conference on Human Factors in Computing Systems, pp. 2767–2770 (2012)
4. Seto, Y., Noguchi, Tosaka, M., Inoue, T.: Development of an another dish re-commender based on dining activity recognition, Technical Report. The Institute of Electronics, Information and Communication Engineers 107(554), 55–60 (2008)
5. Narumi, T., Ban, Y., Kajinami, T., Tanikawa, T., Hirose, M.: Augmented perception of satiety: controlling food consumption by changing apparent size of food with augmented reality. In: Proceedings of the ACM-CHI Conference on Human Factors in Computing Systems, pp. 109–118 (2012)
6. Mukawa, N., Tokunaga, H., Yuasa, M., Tsuda, Y., Tateyama, K., Kasamatsu, C.: Analysis on Utterance Behaviors Embedded in Eating Actions: How are Conversations and Hand-Mouth-Motions Controlled in Three-Party Table Talk? The Institute of Electronics, Information and Communication Engineers (A) J94-A(7), 500–508 (2011)
7. Inoue, T., Otake, M.: Effect of meal in triadic table talk: Equalization of speech and gesture between participants. Transactions of Human Interface Society 13(3), 19–29 (2011)
8. Furukawa, D., Inoue, T.: Showing meal in video-mediated table talk makes conversation close to face-to-face. Journal of Information Processing Society of Japan 54(1), 266–274 (2013)

9. Nawahdah, M., Inoue, T.: Virtually dining together in time-shifted environment: KIZUNA design. In: Proceedings of the 13th ACM Conference on Computer-Supported Cooperative Work, pp. 779–788 (2013)

10. Higaki, Y., Furukawa, D., Inoue, T.: Difference in face-to-face dyadic conversation behavior on uneven meal distribution settings. Technical Report, The Institute of Electronics, Information and Communication Engineers 113(72), 91–96 (2013)

11. Enomoto, M., Ishizaki, M., Koiso, H., Den, Y., Mizukami, E., Yano, H.: A Statistical Investigation of Basic Units for Spoken Interaction Analysis, Technical Report. The Institute of Electronics, Information and Communication Engineers 104(445), 45–50 (2004) (in Japanese)

12. Mizukami, E., Yano, H.: The Structure of Inter-Pausal Unit in Dialogue, Technical Report. The Japanese Society for Artificial Intelligence, Special Interest Group on Spoken Language Understanding and Dialogue Processing 39, 43–48 (2003)

13. Weizenbaum, J.: ELIZA: A computer program for the study of natural language communication between man and machine. Communications of the ACM 9(1), 36–45 (1966)

14. Reeves, E., Nass, C.: The media equation: How people treat computers, television, and new media like real people and places. The Center for the Study of Language and Information Publications (1996)

15. Shibusawa, S., Huang, H., Hayashi, Y., Kawagoe, K.: An Empirical Analysis on the Relationship of Mood and Attitude between Talkers during Active Listening: Toward Active Listening Agent for the Elderly, Technical Report. The Institute of Electronics, Information and Communication Engineers, Human Communication Society 2012-75, 125–129 (2013) (in Japanese)

16. Wada, K., Shibata, T.: Living with seal robots: Its socio-psychological and physiological influences on the elderly in a care house. IEEE Transactions on Robotics and Mechatronics 19(6), 691–697 (2007)

17. Kobayashi, Y., et al.: Design targeting voice interface robot capable of active listening. In: Proceedings of the 5th ACM/IEEE International Conference on Human-robot Interaction, pp. 161–162 (2010)

18. Watanabe, T., et al.: InterActor: Speech-Driven Embodied Interactive Actor. International Journal of Human - Computer Interaction 17(1), 43–60 (2004)

19. Richardson, J.T.E.: Handbook of qualitative research methods for psychology and the social sciences. Wiley-Blackwell (April 1996)

A Study of Changing Locations of Vibrotactile Perception on a Forearm by Visual Stimulation

Arinobu Niijima and Takefumi Ogawa

The University of Tokyo, Japan
a.niijima@ogawa-lab.org,
ogawa@nc.u-tokyo.ac.jp
http://www.ogawa-lab.org

Abstract. In order to interact with virtual objects, presenting tactile stimulation as if a user touched them is very important. Most previous works employ tactile devices such as vibration actuators. However, the system can present tactile stimulation only where the tactile devices are attached. Thus, it has been difficult to present tactile stimulation where the devices are not attached. In this paper, we propose a method to change the location of vibrotactile perception by visual stimulation for extending the area where we can present tactile stimulation. We conducted experiments to investigate influence of visual stimulation on vibrotactile perception, and observed that subjects felt the location of vibrotactile perception shifted to that of the presented virtual object when they were on different locations.

Keywords: augmented reality, vibrotactile perception, cross modal, phantom sensation.

1 Introduction

In augmented reality environment, tactile feedback is important for rich interaction with virtual objects [1, 2]. There have been studies on tactile feedback in order to improve interaction with virtual objects [3, 4]. They employed some actuators such as vibration motors to present tactile feedback. In addition, to present tactile stimulation where actuators are not attached, some researchers employ phantom sensation [5–8]. Phantom sensation is one of tactile illusion, which presents vibrotactile perception between two spatially separated vibration actuators [9, 10]. Both location and intensity of phantom sensation can be controlled by the intensities of physical actuators simultaneously. If the intensities of two actuators are different, the location of phantom sensation will be shifted towards that of the actuator with higher intensity. However, the presentable area of phantom sensation is limited on the line between two actuators [11, 12]. Furthermore, the spatial resolution of vibrotactile perception is low so that users cannot feel the exact location of tactile stimulation clearly [13, 14].

In our study, we propose a method to control locations of vibrotactile perception utilizing visual stimulation such as virtual objects presented by augmented

T. Yuizono et al. (Eds.): CollabTech 2014, CCIS 460, pp. 86–95, 2014.

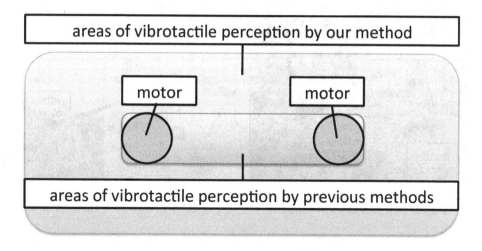

Fig. 1. The difference of our proposal method and previous methods

reality. It is based on previous works which confirmed visual stimulation influence tactile perception (cross modal) [15–18]. Our aim is to change the locations of vibrotactile perception by cross modal using visual stimulation. In this paper, we describe the detail of the method to extend areas of vibrotactile perception by visual stimulation, and some experiments to investigate the feasibility.

2   Our Approach

According to previous woks and pilot study, it seemed to be difficult to perceive exact locations of tactile stimulation on a forearm [6, 8]. Therefore, we assumed that visual stimulation can change the locations of vibrotactile perception on a forearm because cross modal between visual and tactile perception occurs when they are presented simultaneously [15–18]. Based on this, we set a following hypothesis;

- The location of vibrotactile perception is shifted to that of visual stimulation by presenting visual stimulation and tactile stimulation on different locations when the distance of them is below a certain threshold.

In previous works which used phantom sensation, the presentable areas of vibrotactile perception are limited on the line between two vibration actuators. However, our proposal method, which utilizes cross modal by visual stimulation, can present vibrotactile perception out of the line between the actuators as shown in Figure 1. This method is useful to present tactile feedback in large areas with a few vibration motors.

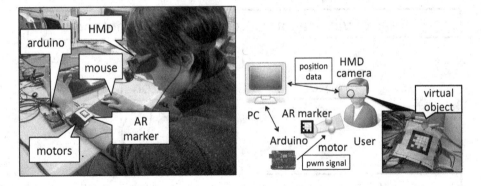

Fig. 2. Experimental environment   **Fig. 3.** Architecture of the system

3   Experiment

To verify our proposal method, we conducted following experiments. In experiment 1, we verified the difference of vibrotactile perception by phantom sensation and that by direct stimulation. In experiment 2, we verified the influence of visual stimulation on the location of vibrotactile perception by presenting a virtual object. In experiment 3, we investigated the distance under which visual stimulation influences the locations of vibrotactile perception strongly. In experiment 4, we investigated the change of vibrotactile perception by visual stimulation on a plane whose size was 40×40 mm^2.

The experimental environment was shown in Figure 2 . The architecture of the system was shown in Figure 3. We used ARToolkit for presenting a virtual ball as visual stimulation [19], and coin-type vibration motors (FM34F) with diameter of 10 mm for tactile stimulation. Arduino was used to control the power of the motors [20]. Subjects wore HMD (Vuzix Wrap 920) to look at their own left forearm.

3.1   Experiment 1: Verification of Phantom Sensation

Method. Four subjects (26-37 years old; four males) participated in this experiment. They were equipped with nine vibration motors on the left forearm as shown in Figure 4. The distance of each motors was 20 mm, which is seemed to be suitable for presenting phantom sensation from pilot study. The motors were supplied with 3.0 V and the frequency of the vibration was about 200 Hz. The vibration patterns were 45 patterns, which include 9 patterns stimulated by one motor and 36 patterns stimulated by two motors. The motors vibrated for 1.0 s and the interval of the next vibration was 1.0 s.

The vibration pattern was selected randomly. Subjects answered the locations of vibrotactile perception by clicking on a window, on which they looked at their arms, with a mouse. The distance between the location of vibrotactile perception

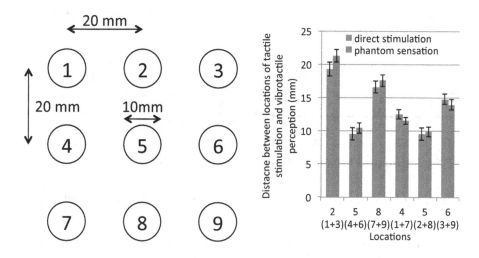

Fig. 4. Layout of motors   **Fig. 5.** Result of experiment 1

and that of tactile stimulation was recorded. The number of trials for each subject was 500.

Result and Discussion. We calculated the average distance between the location of vibrotactile perception and that of tactile stimulation when the tactile stimulation was on the locations "2, 4, 5, 6, 8" in Figure 4. Figure 5 shows the distance when each location was stimulated directly by one motor or stimulated by phantom sensation from two motors. For example, the location "2" was stimulated by one motor whose location was "2" and by two motors whose locations were "1, 3". Only on the location "5", the distance was calculated by three vibration patterns; "5", "4, 6", "2, 8".

This result shows the distance by two vibration patterns was little different. We conducted t-test in each location to investigate significant difference. In all locations, there were no significant difference. Therefore, it is useful to use phantom sensation instead of stimulating by a vibration motor directly.

3.2 Experiment 2: The Influence of Visual Stimulation on the Locations of Vibrotactile Perception

Method. In this experiment, we used two motors whose distance was 40 mm. The motors were supplied with voltage from 2.25 V to 3.0 V under control of Arduino. Frequency of the vibrations was about from 200 Hz to 250 Hz, which is suited to present tactile stimulation [9]. The latency of the motors was about 100 ms. Tactile stimulation was presented on five locations whose interval was 10 mm. The locations were set according to the distance from the left motor as following; 0 mm, 10 mm, 20 mm, 30 mm, and 40 mm as shown in Figure 6. The voltage of two motors was changed as following; (distance from left motor, voltage of left motor,

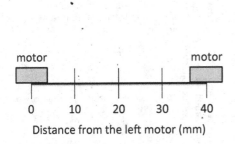

Fig. 6. Locations of tactile stimulation

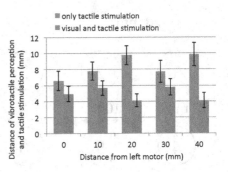

Fig. 7. Result of experiment 2

voltage of right motor) = (0 mm, 3.0 V, 0 V), (10 mm, 2.75 V, 2.25 V), (20 mm, 2.5 V, 2.5 V), (30 mm, 2.25 V, 2.75 V), (40 mm, 0 V, 3.0 V).

Seven subjects (23-37 years old; five males and two females) participated in this experiment. First, tactile stimulation was presented without visual stimulation. Subjects answered the locations of vibrotactile perception with a mouse, then next position was selected and stimulated randomly. We informed them the number of motors, but we did not inform them the vibration patterns. The number of trials was 50. We measured the distance between the locations of tactile stimulation and vibrotactile perception. Next, we presented not only tactile stimulation but also a virtual ball whose radius was 5 mm on the same location of the tactile stimulation. We did not inform them that visual stimulation and tactile stimulation were presented on the same location. We compared the distance between the location of vibrotactile perception and that of tactile stimulation under each condition.

Result and Discussion. Figure 7 shows the result of experiment 2. In all positions, the distance between the locations of vibrotactile perception and tactile stimulation became shorter when the tactile stimulation was presented with visual stimulation than when only tactile stimulation was presented. The average distance was about 5 mm, which was the same as the radius of the virtual ball, when both stimulation was presented. It is appeared that visual stimulation helped subjects perceive the exact location of tactile stimulation clearly. Based on this, we confirmed that visual stimulation can influence the locations of vibrotactile perception.

3.3 Experiment 3: The Distance under Which Visual Stimulation Influences the Location of Vibrotactile Perception

Method In this experiment, we used two motors as experiment 2. The locations of tactile stimulation were also the same. The virtual ball was presented on different location, which was on the line between two motors, from that of tactile

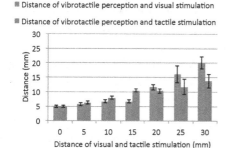

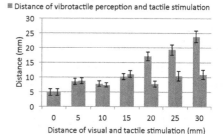

Fig. 8. Result of experiment 3 (same)   **Fig. 9.** Result of experiment 3 (different)

stimulation. The distance between the locations of tactile stimulation and the virtual ball was set as 0 mm, 5 mm, 10 mm, 15 mm, 20 mm, 25 mm, and 30 mm.

Seven subjects (23-37 years old; five males and two females) participated in this experiment. Subjects answered the locations of vibrotactile perception. We informed them that the locations of visual and tactile stimulation were not always the same. The number of trials was 100. The other conditions were the same in the experiment 2. We measured the distance between the locations of tactile stimulation and vibrotactile perception. We also measured that of visual stimulation and vibrotactile perception. In addition, the moving direction of visual stimulation and tactile stimulation were measured, and we classified the results into two patterns; (1) the same moving direction of visual and tactile stimulation, (2) the different moving direction of visual and tactile stimulation. For example, if the location of visual stimulation moved from "0 mm" to "20 mm" in Figure 6, the moving direction of visual stimulation was right. If that of tactile stimulation moved from "10 mm" to "40 mm", the moving direction of tactile stimulation was right. Therefore, it was (1) pattern. If that of tactile stimulation moved from "10 mm" to "0 mm", the moving direction of tactile stimulation was left. Therefore, it was (2) pattern.

Result and Discussion. Figure 8 shows the result of experiment 3 in the case of the same moving direction, and Figure 9 shows the result of experiment 3 in the case of different moving direction. In both cases, when the distance between visual and tactile stimulation was under 15 mm, that between vibrotactile perception and visual stimulation was shorter than that between vibrotactile perception and tactile stimulation. That between vibrotactile perception and visual stimulation was longer and longer over 20 mm of that between visual and tactile stimulation, and that between tactile perception and tactile stimulation became fixed. It means that the influence of visual stimulation appeared under conditions which the distance between visual and tactile stimulation was under 15 mm.

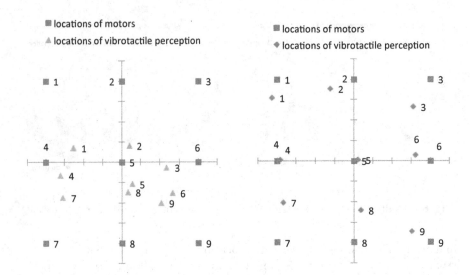

Fig. 10. Locations of vibrotactile percep-   **Fig. 11.** Locations of vibrotactile perception when the virtual ball was not pre-   tion when the virtual ball was presented
sented   on the same location as the tactile stimu-
    lation

On the other hand, the distance between vibrotactile perception and visual stimulation became shorter in the case of the same moving direction than in the case of the different moving direction. Therefore, We confirmed that the influence of visual stimulation became stronger in the case of the same moving direction.

3.4   Experiment 4: Investigation of the Change of the Locations of Vibrotactile Perception by Visual Stimulation

Method Four subjects (24-26 years old; four males) participated in this experiment. They were equipped with nine vibration motors on the left forearm as shown in Figure 4. The vibration patterns were the same as experiment 1. The vibration pattern was selected randomly.

A virtual ball as experiment 2 was presented on the locations from "1" to "9" in Figure 4. It was bounded on the location with 1.0 s interval, and the height was 10 mm. The vibration and the bound of the virtual ball were synchronized. The location of the virtual ball was selected randomly.

Subjects answered the locations of vibrotactile perception by clicking on a window, on which they looked at their arms, with a mouse. The locations of vibrotactile perception, those of visual stimulation, and those of tactile stimulation were recorded. The number of trials was 500.

Result and Discussion. To investigate the influence of the visual stimulation, we used the result of experiment 1. Figure 10 shows the locations of tactile

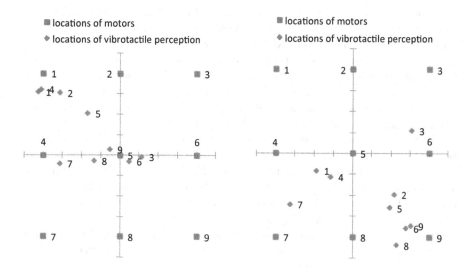

Fig. 12. Locations of vibrotactile perception when the virtual ball was presented on the location "1"

Fig. 13. Locations of vibrotactile perception when the virtual ball was presented on the location "9"

stimulation and vibrotactile perception in experiment 1. Each number of "locations of motors" corresponds with Figure 4. That of "locations of vibrotactile perception" means the average locations of vibrotactile perception when the tactile stimulation was presented on each location. For example, "1" in locations of vibrotactile perception shows that the average location of subjects' vibrotactile perception when tactile stimulation was presented on "1". The locations of vibrotactile perception were gathered around the center. This result corresponds with the knowledge in previous works that spatial resolution of vibrotactile perception is low [13, 14].

Figure 11 shows the locations when the virtual ball was presented on the same location of tactile stimulation. Each distance between the locations of tactile stimulation and vibrotactile perception was shorter than that without the virtual ball. Figure 12 and Figure 13 show the locations when the virtual ball was presented on the location "1" and "9" respectively. Under each condition, the locations of vibrotactile perception were shifted to those of the virtual ball.

According to these results, we confirmed that the location of visual stimulation influences that of vibrotactile perception even on a plane. Therefore, the area of presentable vibrotactile perception seems to be extended by presenting visual stimulation on different location from that of tactile stimulation.

4   Conclusions and Future Works

In augmented reality environment, tactile feedback is important for rich interaction with virtual objects, and the presentable area of vibrotactile perception was limited on the locations of actuators and the line between two actuators. In this paper, we proposed a method to extend the locations of vibrotactile perception by presenting a virtual object whose location is different from that of tactile stimulation. We conducted some experiments to investigate influence of visual stimulation on vibrotactile perception, and observed that subjects felt the location of vibrotactile perception shifted to that of the presented virtual object when they were on different locations. The results showed when the distance between the locations of visual stimulation and tactile stimulation was under 15mm, the influence of visual stimulation appeared strongly so that the location of the vibrotactile perception was shifted to that of visual stimulation. We also confirmed that the influence of visual stimulation became stronger in the case of the same moving direction of visual stimulation and tactile stimulation. Therefore, it seems to be possible to extend the area of presentable vibrotactile perception by controlling the location of visual stimulation.

In future works, we will conduct these experiments with more subjects to verify our proposal method. In addition, we will apply this method on other parts such as a palm. We will also investigate the influence of the size and shape of virtual objects on vibrotactile perception.

Acknowledgement. This research was supported in part by a Grant-in-Aid for Scientific Research (C) numbered 25330227 by the Japan Society for the Promotion of Science (JSPS).

References

1. Biocca, F., Kim, J., Choi, Y.: Visual touch in virtual environments: An exploratory study of presence, multimodal interfaces, and cross-modal sensory illusions. Teleoperators and Virtual Environments 10(3), 247–265 (2001)
2. Lee, S.P., Cheok, A.D., James, T.K.S., Debra, G.P.L., Jie, C.W., Chuang, W., Farbiz, F.: A mobile pet wearable computer and mixed reality system for human-poultry interaction through the internet. Personal and Ubiquitous Computing 10(5), 301–317 (2006)
3. Aoki, T., Mitake, H., Keoki, D., Hasegawa, S., Sato, M.: Wearable haptic device to present contact sensation based on cutaneous sensation using thin wire. In: Proceedings of the International Conference on Advances in Computer Entertainment Technology, pp. 115–122 (2009)
4. Seo, B.-K., Choi, J., Han, J.-H., Park, H., Park, J.-I.: One-handed interaction with augmented virtual objects on mobile devices. In: Proceedings of the 7th ACM SIGGRAPH International Conference on Virtual-Reality Continuum and Its Applications in Industry (2008)
5. Seo, J., Choi, S.: Initial study for creating linearly moving vibrotactile sensation on mobile device. In: IEEE Haptic Symposium, pp. 67–70 (2010)
6. Rahal, L., Cha, J., El Saddik, A., Kammerl, J., Steinbachand, E.: Investigating the influence of temporal intensity changes on apparent movement phenomenon. In: Virtual Environments, Human-Computer Interfaces and Measurements Systems, pp. 310–313 (2009)
7. Ueda, S., Uchida, M., Nozawa, A., Ide, H.: A tactile display using phantom sensation with apparent movement together. Electronics and Communications in Japan 91(12), 29–38 (2008)

8. Barghout, A., Cha, J., El Saddik, A., Kammerl, J., Steinbach, E.: Spatial resolution of vibrotactile perception on the human forearm when exploiting funneling illusion. In: Haptic Audio visual Environments and Games, pp. 19–23 (2009)

9. Alles, D.S.: Information transmission by phantom sensations. IEEE Transactions on Man-Machine Systems 11, 85–91 (1970)

10. Kato, H., Hashimoto, Y., Kajimoto, H.: Basic properties of phantom sensation for practical haptic applications. In: EuroHaptics (2010)

11. Israr, A., Poupyrev, I.: Tactile brush: Drawing on skin with a tactile grid display. In: CHI 2011, pp. 2019–2028 (2011)

12. Yang, G.-H., Jin, M.-S., Jin, Y., Kang, S.: T-mobile: Vibrotactile display pad with spatial and directional information for hand-held device. In: Intelligent Robots and Systems, pp. 5245–5250 (2010)

13. Stevens, J.C., Choo, K.K.: Spatial acuity of the body surface over the life span. Somatosensory and Motor Research 13, 153–166 (1996)

14. Pongrac, H.: Vibrotactile perception: examining the coding of vibrations and the just noticeable difference under various conditions. Multimedia Systems 13, 297–307 (2008)

15. Spence, C., Pavani, F., Driver, J.: Spatial constraints on visual-tactile cross-modal distractor congruency effects. Cognitive, Affective, & Behavioral Neuroscience 4(2), 148–169 (2004)

16. Craig, J.C.: Visual motion interferes with tactile motion perception. Perception 35, 351–367 (2006)

17. Biocca, F.A., Inoue, Y., Lee, A., Polinsky, H., Tang, A.: Visual cues and virtual touch: Role of visual stimuli and intersensory integration in cross-modal haptic illusions and the sense of presence. In: Proceedings of Presence, pp. 376–394 (2002)

18. Sano, Y., Hirano, Y., Kimura, A., Shibata, F., Tamura, H.: Dent-softness illusion in mixed reality space: Further experiments and considerations. In: Proceedings of Virtual Reality, pp. 153–154 (2013)

19. NyARToolKit project, http://nyatla.jp/nyartoolkit/wp/ (retrieved April 15, 2014)

20. Arduino, http://www.arduino.cc/ (retrieved April 15, 2014)

Comparing Video, Avatar, and Robot Mediated Communication: Pros and Cons of Embodiment

Kazuaki Tanaka[1,2], Hideyuki Nakanishi[1], and Hiroshi Ishiguro[3]

[1] Department of Adaptive Machine Systems, Osaka University
2-1 Yamadaoka, Suita, Osaka 565-0871, Japan
{tanaka,nakanishi}@ams.eng.osaka-u.ac.jp
[2] CREST, Japan Science and Technology Agency
[3] Department of Systems Innovation, Osaka University
1-3 Machikaneyama, Toyonaka, Osaka 560-8531, Japan
ishiguro@sys.es.osaka-u.ac.jp

Abstract. In recent years, studies have begun on robot conferencing as a new telecommunication medium. In robot conferencing, people talk with a remote conversation partner through teleoperated robots which present the bodily motions of the partner with a physical embodiment. However, the effects of physical embodiment on distant communication had not yet been demonstrated. In this study, to find the effects, we conducted an experiment in which subjects talked with a partner through robots and various existing communication media (e.g. voice, avatar and video chats). As a result, we found that the physical embodiment enhanced social telepresence, i.e., the sense of resembling face-to-face interaction. Furthermore, the result implied that physical embodiment built the sense of tension as in the case of a first face-to-face meeting.

Keywords: Robot conferencing, physical embodiment, social telepresence, social anxiety, teleconferencing, videoconferencing, audio communication, avatar, face-to-face communication, face tracking.

1 Introduction

Currently, we can easily use audio and videoconferencing software. Audio-only conferencing, such as a voice chat, has a problem in that social telepresence decreases. The social telepresence is the sense of resembling face-to-face interaction [7]. Enhancing social telepresence psychologically makes the physical distance between remote people less and saves time and money on travel. The most common method of enhancing social telepresence is videoconferencing. It had been proposed that live video can transmit the social telepresence of a remote conversation partner [6, 11]. Nevertheless, videoconferencing does not transmit sufficient social telepresence compared with face-to-face conferencing.

To further enhance social telepresence, recent studies have begun on robot conferencing in which people talk with a remote conversation partner through teleoperated robots. The teleoperated robot uses motion tracking technologies to reflect partner's

T. Yuizono et al. (Eds.): CollabTech 2014, CCIS 460, pp. 96–110, 2014.
© Springer-Verlag Berlin Heidelberg 2014

facial and body motions in real time. The main features of robot conferencing are to transmit conversation partner's body motions and to present these motions via a physical embodiment. The physical embodiment means the substitution of a partner's body that exists physically in the same place as a user. Thus, it is expected that the user can talk with feeling close to face-to-face. Some studies reported superiorities of robot conferencing to videoconferencing [15, 22]. One such study showed that the teleoperated robot which has a realistic human appearance enhances social telepresence compared with audio-only conferencing and videoconferencing [22]. Even so, it is difficult that each user owns a robot with his/her realistic appearance due to the high cost. For this reason, a teleoperated robot that has a humanlike face without a specific age or gender is developed [21]. However, it has not been yet found whether such an anonymous robot that transmits only body motions without disclosing an appearance still has superiority to videoconferencing.

As the communication medium similar to the robot conferencing, avatar chats are available. Recently, it has become easy and inexpensive to use avatar chats such as avatar Kinect. The avatar chat resembles the robot conferencing in transmitting user's body motions without disclosing the user's appearance, but differs in reflecting these movements onto a computer graphics animation which does not have a physical embodiment. A lot of studies found positive effects of avatar on distant communication [2, 4, 8, 12, 25]. Several such studies reported that avatar chats enhance social telepresence compared with audio-only conferencing [4, 12]. In addition, it was also reported that avatars increase the degree of smoothness of speech as well as video conferencing [25]. Thus, the transmitting body motions might be enough to produce these positive effects. If the physical embodiment does not produce such positive effects, the usefulness of robot conferencing would decrease since robots are more expensive than videos and avatars.

Therefore, to prove that robot conferencing is useful, it is necessary to demonstrate that the physical embodiment improves distant communication independently from the transmitting information, e.g., audio, motion and appearance. In this study, we investigated how the physical embodiment and transmitting information factors influence the social telepresence and the degree of smoothness of speech. To analyze the effects of the two factors separately, we prepared six communication methods as shown in Fig. 1. The voice chat, avatar chat and videoconferencing that do not have a physical embodiment transmit audio only, audio + motion and audio + motion + appearance respectively. The robot conferencing that has a physical embodiment transmits audio + motion, and so it corresponds to the avatar chat as described above. As the method that corresponds to the voice chat, we set an inactive robot conferencing that transmits audio but no motion. Furthermore, we assumed that the face-to-face communication corresponds to the videoconferencing.

2   Related Work

There are many studies related to robot conferencing. They have proposed various teleoperated robots that present the operator's facial movements [13, 15, 21, 22, 24] with a physical embodiment. A previous study that evaluated robot conferencing with regard to social telepresence concluded that robot conferencing transmitted a higher social telepresence of the remote conversation partner than audio-only and videoconferencing [22]. However, the teleoperated robot that was used in the study had a specific person's appearance, and so it was not clear which of the factors, the physical embodiment or the appearance, enhanced the social telepresence. Additionally, the teleoperated robot reproduced the whole body of a person, whereas the videoconferencing only showed conversational partner's head. The video image of only a head is harmful to social telepresence [20], so that a superiority of robot conferencing to videoconferencing which shows the whole body of a person was also not clear. To clarify them, we used an anonymous teleoperated robot [21] that has a humanlike face without a specific age or gender, and compared it with life-size communication media that reproduced the whole body of the conversational partner.

In videoconferencing research, it was reported that the remote person's movement that was augmented by a display's physical movement enhanced the social telepresence [18]. Furthermore, in the human-robot interaction field, there are studies that focused on the effects of the physical embodiment of robot agents on social presence [3, 14]. These studies showed that people feel higher social presence from robot agents than on-screen agents. There is a possibility that people also feel higher social telepresence during robot conferencing due to the effects of the physical embodiment.

The superiority of robot conferencing to videoconferencing was indicated also in objective measures. One such study showed that the eye-gaze of remote person reproduced by a robot was more recognizable than by a live-video [15]. Most previous studies that tried to find influences of a difference between communication media on objective measures have focused on conversational structures such as turn-taking and overlapping [1, 5, 23]. In this study, we observed the frequency of pauses and percentage of pause times in speech to measure the degree of smoothness of speech [25]. The concrete methods to calculate them are explained in Section 3.4.

The previous studies that showed superiorities of robot conferencing dealt with each telecommunication media as a single factor [15, 22]. By contrast, this study divided the telecommunication media into a physical embodiment factor and a transmitting information factor. For example, we assumed that a robot has a physical embodiment and transmits audio and body motions, and a video does not have a physical embodiment and transmits audio, body motions and appearances.

3   Experiment

3.1   Hypothesis

In this study, we conducted an experiment to confirm how features of robot conferencing influence distant communication. The main features of robot conferencing are to have a physical embodiment and to transmit conversation partner's body motions. We predicted that these features enhance social telepresence, and so we made the following two hypotheses.

Hypothesis 1: A physical embodiment enhances the social telepresence of the conversation partner.

Hypothesis 2: Transmitting body motions enhances the social telepresence of the conversation partner.

The previous study that investigated the influence of difference between communication media on the degree of smoothness of speech showed that body motions presented by videos and avatars decreased speech pauses compared with audio-only media [25]. In addition, it was reported that videos and avatars enhance social telepresence compared with audio-only media [4, 12]. On the assumption that enhancing social telepresence smoothens speeches, we predicted that the features of robot conferencing could decrease speech pauses. Thus, we added the following two hypotheses.

Hypothesis 3: A physical embodiment smoothens a speech that is directed to the remote conversation partner.

Hypothesis 4: Transmitting body motions smoothens a speech that is directed to the remote conversation partner.

3.2   Conditions

The hypotheses described in the preceding section consist of these two factors: physical embodiment and transmitting information. The physical embodiment factor had two levels, with/without physical embodiment, and the transmitting information factor had three levels, audio, audio + motion and audio + motion + appearance. Thus, to examine the hypotheses, we prepared six conditions of a 2x3 design shown in Fig. 1.

As described in Section 1, both robot conferencing and avatar chat transmit remote person's body motions without disclosing the person's appearance. We thus supposed that the avatar chat can become robot conferencing by adding a physical embodiment. Similarly, we assumed that the voice chat becomes an inactive robot conferencing which does not transmit the body motions of a remote person and the video chat can become face-to-face communication by adding a physical embodiment. In terms of the transmitting information, we assumed that the voice chat and inactive robot transmit only audio, the avatar and robot transmit audio and motion, and the video and face-to-face transmit audio, motion and appearance. These assumptions allowed us to analyze the effect of adding a physical embodiment to existing communication media. The details of each condition are described below.

Active Robot Condition (Transmitting Audio and Motion with a Physical Embodiment): The subject talked to the conversation partner while looking at the robot. The robot had a three-degrees-of-freedom neck and a one-degree-of-freedom mouth. The head and lips moved at thirty frames per second according to the sensor data sent from face tracking software (faceAPI), that was running in a remote terminal and capturing the conversation partner's movements. The camera for face tracking was set behind the robot. The microphone speaker was set behind the robot. The robot was dressed with the same gray shirt as the conversation partner.

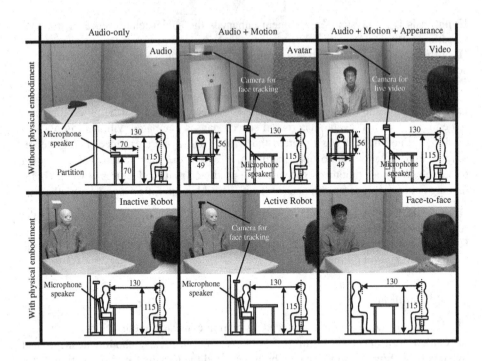

Fig. 1. Experimental conditions and setups (length unit: centimeters)

Avatar Condition (Transmitting Audio and Motion But No Physical Embodiment):

The subject talked to the conversation partner while looking at an anonymous three-dimensional computer graphics avatar that reflected the conversation partner's head and lip motions. The avatar consisted of a skin-colored cylindrical head, black lips, black eyeballs and a gray conical body which was the same color as the shirt of the conversation partner. In the preliminary experiment, we used an avatar which had a spherical head and a realistic shirt, which looked like the robot. However there were some subjects who felt hard to notice facial movements of the avatar. This problem was solved by changing the design of avatar to a cylindrical head. The recognizable facial movements might improve social telepresence, and so we employed the cylindrical head. In addition, we modified its body to a conical shape to standardize the abstraction level of the looks. The diameter of the head was equal to the breadth of the robot's head (13.5 cm). The conversation partner's head and lip motions were tracked in the same way as on the active robot condition. The head translated and rotated with three degrees of freedom. The lips were transformed based on the three-dimensional positions of fourteen markers. The head and lips moved at thirty frames per second. The avatar was shown on a 40-inch display. The display was set longitudinally on the other side of the desk. The bezel of the display was covered with a white board, so that the true display area was 49 cm by 56 cm. The microphone speaker was set behind the display. There were two cameras on top of the display. One was for face tracking, and the other was for live video. In this condition, the camera for live video was covered with a white box. The camera was used in the video condition described below.

Face-to-Face Condition (Transmitting Audio, Motion and Appearance with a Physical Embodiment): The subject talked to the conversation partner in a normal face-to-face environment. The conversation partner wore a gray shirt. The distance from the subject to the conversation partner was adjusted to 150 cm so that the breadth of the conversation partner's head looked the same as the breadth of the robot's head (13.5 cm).

Video Condition (Transmitting Audio, Motion and Appearance But No Physical Embodiment): This condition was identical to a normal video chat. The subject talked to the conversation partner while looking at a live video of the conversation partner. The conversation partner wore a gray shirt. The resolution of the camera for live video was 1280 pixels by 720 pixels, and its frame rate was 30 frames per second. The video was shown on the same display that was used in the avatar condition. Thus, the true display area was 49 cm by 56 cm. The horizontal angle of view was adjusted to 87 degrees so that the breadth of the conversation partner's head was equal to the breadth of the robot's head (13.5 cm) on the display. The camera for face tracking that was used on the avatar condition was covered with a white box.

Inactive Robot Condition (Transmitting Audio with a Physical Embodiment): The subject talked to the conversation partner while looking at the inactive robot. The camera for face tracking that was used on the active robot condition was covered with a white box. The subject was preliminarily informed that the robot did not move in this condition.

Audio-Only Condition (Transmitting Audio But No Physical Embodiment): This condition was similar to a normal voice chat. The subject talked to the conversation partner through only a microphone speaker that was set on the desk.

In the preliminary experiment, some subjects doubted that the experimenter would be looking at them from somewhere even if the experimental condition required no camera. We hence informed the subjects that the dialogue environments of the subject side and the conversation partner side were the same in all the conditions. To make the subjects believe this bi-directionality of the dialogue environments, the subjects were shown a live video of the subjects' avatar, robot or video which were seen by the conversation partner on a 7-inch display before each experiment. At the same time, the subjects confirmed that their avatar and robot reflected their face and lip movements. The subjects also confirmed that the avatar and robot in front of them reflected the conversation partner's face and lip movements by comparing a live video of the conversation partner that was shown on the 7-inch display with the avatar and robot. The 7-inch display for these confirmations was removed before the experiments.

3.3   Task

In the experiment, the subject talked with the conversation partner in the six conditions described above. An experimenter played the role of the partner. To observe the difference in the social telepresence between the conditions, we asked the subject to answer a questionnaire (which is explained in the next section) after the experiment ended. Additionally, we observed the speech pauses. It therefore was necessary to record extended speech, which was required to stably measure the speech pauses. Simultaneously, it was also necessary to avoid analyzing speech that was interleaved with a remote conversation partner's replies to the subject, because those replies would become noise that affected the following utterances of the subject. To collect such speech, we created a task in which the subject could continue to talk for more than one minute without the partner's interference. While the subject was talking, the experimenter did not talk and gave only minimum backchannel responses with an utterance and a small nod of his head.

The subject was asked by the experimenter to talk about the issue and resolution of a certain gadget and requests for a new function on that gadget at the beginning of each condition. Because all the subjects had to experience the six conditions, we prepared six gadgets as conversational topics, i.e., e-book readers, handheld game consoles, smartphones, robotic vacuum cleaners, portable audio players, and 3D televisions. We did not disclose the next topic beforehand, and the experimenter told the subject which gadget to talk about right when the condition began.

We did not ask the subject to talk for more than a certain duration, so the subject could stop talking anytime. However, since the six gadgets are attracting considerable attention recently, most subjects knew the issue and resolution of the gadgets to a certain level, and their speech was able to last more than one minute. A one-minute speech would be too short to analyze turn-taking, but it was enough to observe the difference in the pauses.

The order of experiencing the conditions and the order of the topics were counterbalanced. The subject trained the task in the face-to-face condition in order to familiarize the subject with the task and the experimenter's motion and appearance, before conducting the experiment in the six conditions. The topic of the training was always railway smart cards.

3.4   Data Collection

Questionnaire

After experiencing the six conditions, the subjects answered a questionnaire, which asked them to estimate the social telepresence, i.e., the degree of resembling face-to-face interaction [7] for each condition. The questionnaire is shown in Fig. 2. The questionnaire had six statements that corresponded to the six conditions. The statement was the following: I felt as if I were talking to the conversation partner in the same room. Previous studies showed that the statement which asks a feeling of being in the same room is useful to measure the social telepresence [16, 17, 18, 19]. The statement was rated on a 9-point Likert scale where 1 = strongly disagree, 3 = disagree, 5 = neutral, 7 = agree, and 9 = strongly agree. The subjects thereby could score the same number on the statements if they felt the same level of social telepresence in the conditions.

I felt as if I were talking to the conversation partner in the same room.

	strongly disagree	disagree	neutral	agree	strongly agree
	1	2	3	4	5
Inactive	strongly disagree	disagree	neutral	agree	strongly agree
	1	2	3	4	5
	strongly disagree	disagree	neutral	agree	strongly agree
	1	2	3	4	5
Active	strongly disagree	disagree	neutral	agree	strongly agree
	1	2	3	4	5
	strongly disagree	disagree	neutral	agree	strongly agree
	1	2	3	4	5
	strongly disagree	disagree	neutral	agree	strongly agree
	1	2	3	4	5

Fig. 2. Questionnaire to evaluate the social telepresence

The statements were sorted in the order of the conditions and were printed on the questionnaire, with a photo that showed the experimental setup of the corresponding condition. The sort and the photo were good cues to help the subjects remember the feeling of social telepresence in each condition. After answering the questionnaire, the subjects were interviewed. The interview was conducted in order to ask the subjects the reason of scoring of the questionnaire.

Speech Pauses

To calculate the frequency of pauses and the percentage of pause times in the recorded speech, the speech was transcribed by using a multimedia annotation tool, ELAN, which can partially repeat recorded speech and show its waveform. The waveform was good cue to discriminate between pause parts and utterance parts. Three experimenters used this tool for the transcription and the pause estimation. We entered the beginning time, ending time, and transcript of all the utterances to count the pauses.

To exclude arbitrariness from the analysis, we did not have any minimum or maximum threshold for the length of a pause to be counted. However, we could not count a pause that was shorter than fifty milliseconds, because it was actually impossible to distinguish such a short pause from a speaking part due to white noise. We did not filter out white noise, because the filtering could also cut off utterances spoken very quietly. The quiet utterances sometimes mixed with white noise. In such a case, we listened to the part over and over again, shifting the beginning and ending time of the part in steps of ten milliseconds. As a result, we estimated pause parts and utterance parts as accurately as possible. The transcription which was made by one person was checked by two people to confirm the consistency of the pause estimation. In addition, when there were discrepancies in the pause estimation among us, we had ample discussions about it.

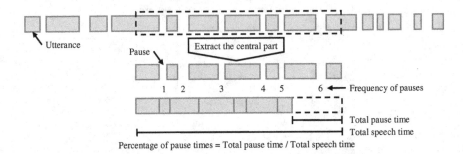

Percentage of pause times = Total pause time / Total speech time

Fig. 3. Method to calculate the frequency of pauses and the percentage of pause times

Fig. 3 shows the method for calculating the frequency of pauses and the percentage of pause times. First, we extracted the central part of the speech. The speech of most subjects lasted more than one minute, which corresponded to about two-hundred syllables in our language (Japanese). Thus, we extracted the central two hundred syllables of the speech for the analysis. This extraction equalized the amount of speech data across conditions and subjects. This extraction also stabilized the analysis, since the pauses of the beginning or ending part of the speech was affected by individual subjects. The beginning part tended to be unfairly smooth if the subject was accidentally ready to talk about the gadget. For example, one subject was considering the purchase of the gadget. Further, the ending part tended to needlessly increase the pauses if the subject made an extra effort to continue talking.

Next, we counted the number of pauses included in the central part. The frequency of pauses is the number. And, we calculated the total speech time and total pause time in the central part. The percentage of pause times was calculated by dividing the total pause time by the total speech time. We used a spreadsheet software to count the number of syllables, extract the central part, count the number of pauses, and calculate the total speech time and total pause time.

4   Result

Thirty-six undergraduate students who lived near our university campus participated in the experiment and talked about the gadgets in the six conditions. Thus, we collected thirty-six questionnaires and 216 recorded speech in total. We analyzed their answers of the questions and speech pauses. The results of analysis are described below.

4.1   Social Telepresence

Fig. 4 shows the result of the questionnaire, in which each point represents the mean value of the scores, and each bar represents the standard error of the mean value.

We compared the six conditions to find the effects of the physical embodiment and the transmitting information factors. Since the physical embodiment and the transmitting information factors consisted of two and three levels as shown in Fig. 1 and each subject evaluated all conditions, we conducted 2x3 two-way repeated-measures

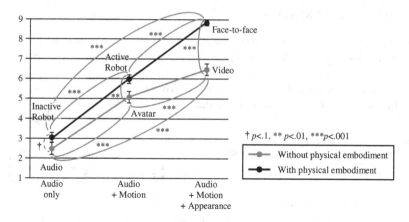

Fig. 4. Results of the questionnaire on the feeling of speaking to the partner in the same room

ANOVA. As a result, we found strong main effects of the physical embodiment factor ($F(1, 35)=36.955$, $p<.001$) and the transmitting information factor ($F(2, 70)=279.603$, $p<.001$). We also found a strong interaction between these factors ($F(2, 70)=14.794$, $p<.001$). We further analyzed the simple main effects in the interaction with the Bonferroni correction. The physical embodiment significantly improved the social telepresence of the conversation partner, when the transmitting information was audio + motion + appearance ($F(1, 105)=8.857$, $p<.01$), and audio + motion ($F(1, 105)=65.470$, $p<.001$). When the transmitting information was audio only, there was a non-significant tendency for the social telepresence to increase ($F(1, 105)=3.460$, $p=.086$). This meant that the subjects felt a higher social telepresence of the conversation partner in the face-to-face condition than in the video condition, and the active robot condition conveyed a higher social telepresence than the avatar. These results support hypothesis 1 that the physical embodiment enhances the social telepresence of the conversation partner. However, the effect of the physical embodiment on the social telepresence was low in the audio only communication.

Furthermore, there were significant differences between the three levels of the transmitting information in both cases of without physical embodiment ($F(2, 140)=223.095$, $p<.001$) and with physical embodiment ($F(2, 140)=107.141$, $p<.001$). Multiple comparisons showed that the subjects felt a higher social telepresence in the face-to-face condition than in the active robot ($p<.001$) and inactive robot ($p<.001$) conditions, the active robot condition conveyed a higher social telepresence than the inactive robot condition ($p<.001$), the video condition conveyed a higher social telepresence than the avatar ($p<.001$) and the audio-only ($p<.001$) conditions, and the avatar condition conveyed a higher social telepresence than the audio-only condition ($p<.001$). These results prove hypothesis 2 that transmitting body motions enhances the social telepresence of the conversation partner. In addition, transmitting appearance also enhances the social telepresence of the conversation partner.

4.2   Smoothness of Speech

In the experiment, most subjects could continue talking for more than one minute, but 10 subjects could not in a few conditions. To calculate the frequency of pauses and the percentage of pause times, we had to extract the central part of the speech because the beginning or ending part of the speech was affected by individual subjects as described in Section 3.4. The speech of less than one minute was too short to extract the

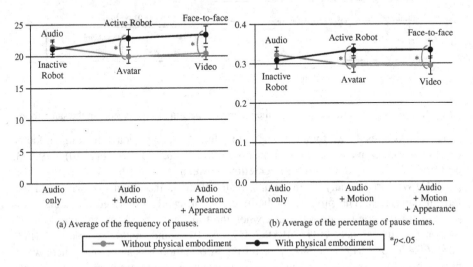

(a) Average of the frequency of pauses.   (b) Average of the percentage of pause times.

— Without physical embodiment   — With physical embodiment   *$p<.05$

Fig. 5. Results of analyzing the speech pauses

central part. We therefore analyzed the pauses of twenty-six subjects who spoke for more than one minute in all the conditions.

Fig. 5(a) and (b) shows the mean value of the frequency of pauses and the percentage of pause times respectively, in which each point represents the mean value. To find the effects of the physical embodiment and the transmitting information factors on the frequency of pauses and the percentage of pause times, we conducted 2x3 two-way repeated-measures ANOVA in the same way as in the result of the questionnaire.

As a result of analyzing the frequency of pauses, we found a strong main effect of the physical embodiment factor ($F(1, 25)=8.004$, $p<.01$), but the main effect of the transmitting information factor was not significant. We also found a weak interaction between these factors ($F(2, 50)=2.947$, $p=.062$). We then analyzed the simple main effects in the interaction with the Bonferroni correction. The physical embodiment significantly increased the frequency of pauses, when the transmitting information was audio + motion + appearance ($F(1, 75)=6.981$, $p<.05$), and audio + motion ($F(1, 75)=6.799$, $p<.05$). There was no other significant effect of the physical embodiment factor.

As a result of analyzing the percentage of pause times, we found a weak main effect of the physical embodiment factor ($F(1, 25)=3.174$, $p=.087$), but the main effect of the transmitting information factor was not significant. We also found a weak interaction between these factors ($F(2, 50)=3.146$, $p=.052$). We then analyzed the simple main effects in the interaction with the Bonferroni correction. The physical embodiment significantly increased the percentage of pause times, when the transmitting information was audio + motion + appearance ($F(1, 75)=4.647$, $p<.05$), and audio + motion ($F(1, 75)=4.369$, $p<.05$). There was no other significant effect of the physical embodiment factor.

These results meant that the subjects' speech included more pauses in the face-to-face condition than in the video condition, and the speech in the active robot condition had more pauses than in the avatar condition, against the hypothesis 3 that a physical embodiment smoothens a speech that is directed to the remote conversation partner. However, the physical embodiment did not influence speech pauses in audio-only communication. Additionally, the transmitting information also did not influence speech pauses, and so the hypothesis 4 that Transmitting body motions smoothens a speech that is directed to the remote conversation partner.

5   Discussion

In the experiment, the physical embodiment enhanced the social telepresence of the conversation partner. In the interviews, seven of the thirty-six subjects said that they felt as if they were facing the conversation partner in the active robot condition compared with the avatar condition because there was a physical object in front of them. However, there was no significant difference between the audio-only condition and the inactive robot condition. In the interviews, three of the thirty-six subjects said that the inactive robot condition was not that different to the audio-only condition because they could not see the conversation partner's reaction. In fact, eight of the thirty-six subjects scored the same number for the audio-only and inactive robot conditions in the questionnaire. Moreover, five of the thirty-six subjects said that they felt as if the conversation partner was in front of them when the robot moved. These subjective responses support the experimental result that a physical embodiment enhances social telepresence when transmitting body motions. This result indicates the superiority of robot conferencing to avatar chat which does not have a physical embodiment.

Presence or absence of motion parallax can be cited as one of the differences between physical embodiment and video. In robot conferencing, the depth from motion parallax could increase visibility of body motions. The lack of the depth information might be the cause of feeling hard to notice facial movements of the avatar used in the preliminary experiment described in Section 3.2. A previous study reported that motion parallax generated by the movement of a camera enhances social telepresence [17]. The visibility of bodily motion improved by the motion parallax may have contributed to enhance social telepresence.

In terms of the transmitting information, the appearance enhanced social telepresence of the conversation partner as well as the body motions. This result shows the disadvantage of robot conferencing and avatar chat that do not transmit the partner's appearance. Although the active robot has this disadvantage, the active robot and video conditions seemed to convey the same degree of social telepresence, as shown in Fig. 4. In the questionnaire, more than half of subjects (sixteen of the thirty-six) scored the same or higher number for the active robot condition than the video condition. We assumed that the enhanced social telepresence by the physical embodiment offset the decreased social telepresence by the absence of the partner's appearance. Therefore, the reported superiority of robot conferencing in the social telepresence to video conferencing [22] could be caused by the robot's realistic appearance.

We predicted that enhancing social telepresence could increase the degree of smoothness of speech. However, against this prediction, the physical embodiment that enhanced social telepresence decreased the degree of smoothness. On the other hand, in Fig. 5(a) and (b), you can see that the frequency of pauses and the percentage of pause times of the avatar and video conditions seemed to be lower than that of the audio-only condition, although the difference was not significant. This could be caused by the effect of decreasing speech pauses by transmitting body motions that was reported in the previous study [25]. We are currently investigating the cause of the non-significance and anticipate that the several differences of experimental environments influenced the speech pauses, e.g. this study used the life-size avatar and video, whereas the previous study used the small-size of them.

The increasing of speech pauses by the physical embodiment might be caused by the sense of tension as in the case of a first face-to-face meeting. In the interviews, sixteen of the thirty-six subjects referred to a sense of tension. Fifteen of the sixteen subjects felt tension in the face-to-face condition, and five of the sixteen subjects felt tension in the active robot condition. By contrast, the subjects who felt tension in the video and avatar conditions were only two of the sixteen subjects respectively, and no subjects felt tension in the inactive robot and audio-only conditions. These subjective responses showed that the subjects felt tension when they could see the conversation partner's motions with a physical embodiment. In the social psychology field, it is known that social anxiety that is the uncomfortable feeling while talking with a conversation partner increases the frequency of pauses [10] and percentage of pause times [9]. We hence considered that the speech pauses in the face-to-face and active robot conditions were increased by social anxiety. The sense of tension when talking with a stranger is one of the social anxieties. Therefore, there is a possibility that robot conferencing builds a sense of tension as in the case of a first face-to-face meeting.

In this study, we did not investigate the conditions that transmit audio and appearance but not motion. Talking through an inactive robot that has a realistic appearance of a partner, and a partner's photo could correspond to such conditions. Watching the partner's photo while talking is a popular situation since many users of instant messengers put their photos in the buddy list. Although the transmitting appearance enhances social telepresence as mentioned above, it has not been clarified whether the appearance works even if the motion is not transmitted. By contrast, the effect of appearance on the smoothness of speech had already demonstrated [25]. The previous study showed that presenting the partner's photo did not increase the degree of smoothness of speech. We hence predict that the appearance also does not enhance social telepresence if the motion is not transmitted as is the case with the physical embodiment. To prove this hypothesis is a future work.

6   Conclusion

In this study, to investigate how the features of robot conferencing influence remote communication, we compared robot conferencing with existing communication media divided into physical embodiment and transmitting information factors. We found that transmitting body motions via the physical embodiment enhances social telepresence. This result shows the superiority of robot conferencing to avatar chat. However, it was also found that presenting conversational partner's appearance which is not transmitted by robot conferencing enhances social telepresence. Consequently, robot conferencing was comparable to videoconferencing since the positive effect of the physical embodiment offset the negative effect of lacking appearance.

Previous studies have discussed the superiority of robot conferencing to videoconferencing. However, we conclude that robot conferencing in the absence of presenting remote person's appearance does not always have the superiority in social telepresence.

In addition, we analyzed the subjects' speech to examine how the physical embodiment and transmitting information factors affect the degree of smoothness of speech. As a result, we also found that transmitting body motions via the physical embodiment increases pauses in speech. This result implies the possibility that robot conferencing builds a sense of tension as in the case of the first face-to-face meeting because the increasing of pauses in speech might be caused by the sense of tension. Thus, robot conferencing could be suitable for interactions that require a sense of tension, e.g., interviews and lectures.

Acknowledgments. This study was supported by JSPS Grants-in-Aid for Scientific Research No. 21680013"Telerobotic media for supporting social telepresence", No. 20220002 "Representation of human presence by using tele-operated androids", JST CREST "Studies on Cellphone-type Teleoperated Androids Transmitting Human Presence" and Global COE Program "Center of Human-friendly Robotics Based on Cognitive Neuroscience."

References

1. Anderson, A.H., Newlands, A., Mullin, J., Fleming, A., Doherty-Sneddon, G., Van Der Velden, J.M.: Impact of Video-Mediated Communication on Simulated Service Encounters. Interacting with Computers 8(2), 193–206 (1996)
2. Bailenson, J.N., Yee, N., Merget, D., Schroeder, R.: The Effect of Behavioral Realism and Form Realism of Real-Time Avatar Faces on Verbal Disclosure, Nonverbal Disclosure, Emotion Recognition, and Copresence in Dyadic Interaction. Presence: Teleoperators & Virtual Environments 15(4), 359–372 (2006)
3. Bainbridge, W.A., Hart, J., Kim, E.S., Scassellati, B.: The benefits of interactions with physically present robots over video-displayed agents. International Journal of Social Robotics 1(3), 41–52 (2011)
4. Bente, G., Ruggenberg, S., Kramer, N.C., Eschenburg, F.: Avatar-Mediated Networking: Increasing Social Presence and Interpersonal Trust in Net-Based Collaborations. Human Communication Research 34(2), 287–318 (2008)
5. Daly-Jones, O., Monk, A.F., Watts, L.: Some Advantages of Video Conferencing over High-quality Audio Conferencing: Fluency and Awareness of Attentional Focus. International Journal of Human-computer Studies 49(1), 21–58 (1998)

6. de Greef, P., Ijsselsteijn, W.: Social Presence in a Home Tele-Application. CyberPsychology & Behavior 4(2), 307–315 (2001)
7. Finn, K.E., Sellen, A.J., Wilbur, S.B.: Video-Mediated Communication. Lawrence Erlbaum Associates (1997)
8. Garau, M., Slater, M., Bee, S., Sasse, M.A.: The Impact of Eye Gaze on Communication Using Humanoid Avatars. In: Proc. CHI 2001, pp. 309–316 (2001)
9. Goberman, A.M., Hughes, S., Haydock, T.: Acoustic characteristics of public speaking: Anxiety and practice effects. Journal of Speech Communication 53(6), 867–876 (2011)
10. Harrigan, J.A., Suarez, I., Hartman, J.S.: Effect of Speech Errors on Observers' Judgments of Anxious and Defensive Individuals. Journal of Research in Personality 28(4), 505–529 (1994)
11. Isaacs, E.A., Tang, J.C.: What Video Can and Can't Do for Collaboration: A Case Study. Multimedia Systems 2(2), 63–73 (1994)
12. Kang, S., Watt, J.H., Ala, S.K.: Communicators' Perceptions of Social Presence as a Function of Avatar Realism in Small Display Mobile Communication Devices. In: Proc. HICSS 2008(2008)
13. Kuzuoka, H., Yamazaki, K., Yamazaki, A., Kosaka, J., Suga, Y., Heath, C.: Dual Ecologies of Robot as Communication Media: Thoughts on Coordinating Orientations and Projectability. In: Proc. CHI 2004, pp. 183–190 (2004)
14. Lee, K.M., Jung, Y., Kim, J., Kim, S.R.: Are physically embodied social agents better than disembodied social agents?: The effects of physical embodiment, tactile interaction, and people's loneliness in human-robot interaction. International Journal of Human-Computer Studies 64(10), 962–973 (2006)
15. Morita, T., Mase, K., Hirano, Y., Kajita, S.: Reciprocal Attentive Communication in Remote Meeting with a Humanoid Robot. In: Proc. ICMI 2007, pp. 228–235 (2007)
16. Nakanishi, H., Murakami, Y., Nogami, D., Ishiguro, H.: Minimum Movement Matters: Impact of Robot-Mounted Cameras on Social Telepresence. In: Proc. CSCW 2008, pp. 303–312 (2008)
17. Nakanishi, H., Murakami, Y., Kato, K.: Movable Cameras Enhance Social Telepresence in Media Spaces. In: Proc. CHI 2009, pp. 433–442 (2009)
18. Nakanishi, H., Kato, K., Ishiguro, H.: Zoom Cameras and Movable Displays Enhance Social Telepresence. In: Proc. CHI 2011, pp. 63–72 (2011)
19. Nakanishi, H., Tanaka, K., Wada, Y.: Remote Handshaking: Touch Enhances Video-Mediated Social Telepresence. In: Proc. CHI 2014, pp. 2143–2152 (2014)
20. Nguyen, D.T., Canny, J.: More than Face-to-Face: Empathy Effects of Video Framing. In: Proc. CHI 2009, pp. 423–432 (2009)
21. Ogawa, K., Nishio, S., Koda, K., Balistreri, G., Watanabe, T., Ishiguro, H.: Exploring the Natural Reaction of Young and Aged Person with Telenoid in a Real World. Journal of Advanced Computational Intelligence and Intelligent Informatics 15(5), 592–597 (2011)
22. Sakamoto, D., Kanda, T., Ono, T., Ishiguro, H., Hagita, N.: Android as a Telecommunication Medium with a Human-like Presence. In: Proc. HRI 2007, pp. 193–200 (2007)
23. Sellen, A.J.: Remote Conversations: The Effects of Mediating Talk with Technology. Human-Computer Interaction 10(4), 401–444 (1995)
24. Sirkin, D., Ju, W.: Consistency in physical and on-screen action improves perceptions of telepresence robots. In: Proc. HRI 2012, pp. 57–64 (2012)
25. Tanaka, K., Onoue, S., Nakanishi, H., Ishiguro, H.: Motion is Enough: How Real-Time Avatars Improve Distant Communication. In: Proc. CTS 2013, pp. 465–472 (2013)

Interacting with 3D Model on Tabletop and Mobile Paper Projection

Yusuke Takeuchi[1,*] and Masanori Sugimoto[2]

[1] Department of Electrical Engineering and Information Systems
University of Tokyo, 7-3-1 Hongo, Bunkyo-ku, Tokyo, Japan
take.yusuke@gmail.com
[2] Department of Computer Science, Hokkaido University
Kita 14, Nishi 9, Kita-ku, Sapporo, Hokkaido, Japan
sugi@ist.hokudai.ac.jp

Abstract. In this paper, we present a system that enables a user to work with a virtual 3D information space on and above a tabletop by combining head-coupled perspective interaction with a mobile paper projection. The mobile paper projection acts as a physical pinhole into the virtual 3D scene. The proposed system is expected to be used for architectural tasks. As it is a work-in-progress study, we describe about the current status of the system and issues to be investigated in our future work.

Keywords: Interaction above a surface, Tabletop platform, Projection on paper, Architecture design task.

1   Introduction

Interaction with virtual 3D models via tabletop surfaces has been investigated and improved by a number of researchers. One major achievement has been the extension of their interaction space from a 2D surface (touch-based interaction) to a 3D space above the surface via intuitive and natural interactions. Extending a tabletop platform to the third dimension should be applicable to many areas, including medicine, education, entertainment, and so on. The system proposed in this paper is expected to be used in the field of architecture design.

An architect develops an idea for a 3D building and presents it to his/her clients. Before presenting the idea, several steps are usually required, such as drawing roughly-sketched blueprints, creating and editing 3D models using CAD software, and building physical architectural models[1]. Much money, time and efforts need to be spent for building architectural models. However, they often have to be modified or even completely rebuilt because of demands from the clients. An architectural model can be used for a range of purposes: to compare its size with surrounding objects, get an idea of how it

---

[*] Currently with IBM Japan.
[1] Personal communications with students in the Department of Architecture, University of Tokyo.

T. Yuizono et al. (Eds.): CollabTech 2014, CCIS 460, pp. 111–118, 2014.

looks from different angles, exhibit it to stakeholders, confirm light and shadow effects, and examine its texture design. Our proposed system is aimed to effectively achieve these various purposes. Two main contributions of this paper are: (1) manipulation techniques for 3D models to be used in architecture design tasks; (2) the integration of 3D visualization, 3D interaction, mobile projection and tabletop systems.

After describing previous research related to this work, we present an overview of our system and its design ideas. Details of the implementation and application scenarios are then described. Finally, we discuss how the system will be extended for collaborative work in our future work.

2   Related Work

2.1   Interaction above a Surface

A 3D object usually has six degrees of freedom (DOF), whereas a multi-touch interface supports only three-DOF manipulations, namely 2D translation on the surface and rotation about the normal vector on the surface. Therefore, multi-touch interaction is not well suited to manipulating 3D objects, which is why the input space for interfaces has been extended recently from a 2D surface to a space above the surface. Hilliges [4] proposes a tabletop system that enables a user to pick up 3D objects based on physics simulations in a 3D scene. The system recognizes a user's hand gesture with a finger-and-thumb circle by processing an IR image. When the user forms the circle with fingers above the surface, the system recognizes it as a 'pickup' gesture, enabling the user to pick up a 3D object. Wilson et al. [11] presents an interactive tabletop system that uses a depth camera to build a height map on the table surface. The height map is used in a driving simulation game that enables players to drive a virtual car over real objects placed on the table. Objects on the surface are captured and reconstructed by the depth camera. The cars and reconstructed 3D objects are controlled by a physics engine, enabling players to build a driving course by folding paper on the surface. In DepthTouch [3], a user can interact with a virtual object with both hands in the 3D space in front of a screen to a multi-touch interface. This work supports head tracking, which enables the user to obtain an immersive experience and to interact in more intuitive manners. By using several calibrated projectors and a depth camera, LightSpace [12] enables several users to interact with digital material, such as pictures, in a large space that includes desks and walls. To enable users to feel immersed in a 3D world, some interactions involve a head-coupled perspective display that renders images on one or more 2D displays with a perspective corrected for the user's view. The idea is based on fish tank virtual reality (FTVR) [10].

Holodesk [5] and Miragetable [2] combine FTVR techniques with 3D interaction. Holodesk is an interactive system combining an optical see-through display and a Kinect camera [1] to create the illusion that users are directly interacting with 3D objects under the screen. In contrast, Miragetable uses a curved projection screen to create a seamless projection on the table surface and the wall. The interaction techniques in both systems are based on 3D reconstruction, user's hand tracking and physics simulation.

2.2   Paper Interfaces

A handheld paper projection screen is a natural and useful interactive interface, and thus has been investigated so far. The mobile projection screen using a paper makes cross-sectional images of projected 3D objects available to a user. Paper Windows [6] presents a prototype windowing environment that simulates the use of digital paper displays. By projecting windows on physical paper with tracking marker, the user can see information, such as web pages or pictures. This work is inspired and motivated through natural manipulations that papers afford and supports a number of interaction methods, which include hold, collocate, collate, flip, rub, staple, point and two-hand pointing. Furthermore, uses can interact with the paper using pens, fingers or other objects by tracking them. Paperlens [8] presents an interactive interface, which uses a handheld paper described as a 'magic lens.' An IR camera and a projector are hung over the user's head. The IR camera tracks the paper in its 6 DOF and IR-reflecting markers are glued to the corners of the rectangular PaperLens to enable detection of the paper's exact rotation and orientation. PaperLens is extended to Tangible Windows [8], which enables to use a paper either as a physical pinhole into a virtual 3D world or as a physical container for part of that world. FlexPad [9] uses Kinect depth data and conducts real-time projection onto 3D deformable surfaces such as an office paper. It can identify hand occlusion based on reflectivity differences from surface materials.

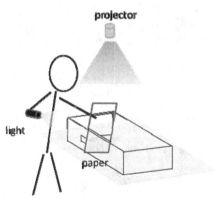

Fig. 1. An overview of the proposed system

3   System Overview

Figure 1 shows an overview of the proposed system. Its tabletop screen shows a 3D model that a user wants to edit or manipulate and its paper screen shows visual or textual information related the projected 3D model on the surface, such as a cross-sectional image or a wire-frame rendering. Each projection provides a user with a correct-perspective view from his/her viewpoint, which is called the head-coupled perspective [10].

The proposed system also supports several interaction techniques that help the user in conducting his/her tasks effectively. Kinect [1] is used to detect a user's head position and capture depth data representing the distance to physical objects such as a user's head or a paper for projection.

By moving the paper, the user can change projected information on its surface, which works as a physical pinhole into a virtual 3D world. Note that the user does not need to wear any devices, such as a head-mounted display or tracking markers. Also, the paper does not require any specific tracking marker - the user can use any hard paper for a physical pinhole window in our system. The proposed system works in the following way: First, all coordinates are unified into one real-world coordinate system by the checkerboard calibration proposed in [13]. After the calibration, 3D models are imported into or created in a 3D scene. Then, Kinect obtains the user's head position and depth data of a paper represented as point clouds, which are transformed from the Kinect coordinate system to the real-world coordinate system. Two Kinect cameras, one directed to the tabletop screen and the other to the paper screen are used and synchronized. When the paper, or the user's head position changes, a correct-perspective image projected on the paper surface is updated immediately. A type of paper projection, such as a cross-sectional image or a wire frame, is chosen by the user depending on a task that he/she is involved.

Fig. 2. System configuration: the Kinect acquires the user's current head position and two projectors are used, for the paper projection and the tabletop projection

4   Implementation

4.1   Configuration

Figure 2 shows the configuration of the proposed system. In addition to two Kinect cameras, two projectors, one for the tabletop projection and the other for the paper projection, are used. To avoid generating shadows because of occlusions, the projector for the tabletop projection is mounted under the surface. The Kinect cameras and the projectors are calibrated, with each coordinate system being unified into one real-world coordinate system [13]. The proposed system is currently implemented for single user. However, because of the nature of architecture design tasks, making the system usable for collaborative work by multiple users is inevitable. How the system will be extended is described in Section 5.

4.2   Correct Perspective

To allow a user to experience a 3D real world using our system, a head-coupled perspective is implemented (some VR displays support stereoscopic rendering of 3D scenes, but we do not focus on this aspect here.) Technically, this is achieved by setting the zero-parallax plane in off-axis perspective projections. The position of a camera in the 3D scene is synchronized with the user's head position and off-axis projections are applied. Instead of a stereoscopic image, we use a monoscopic view whose cues involve relative size, texture gradients, linear perspective, occlusion and motion parallax. By walking around the table, the user can feel immersed in a 3D world. The paper projection also supports a head-coupled perspective, enabling the user to work with the paper and the tabletop simultaneously.

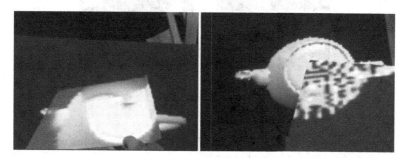

Fig. 3. Left: cross-sectional image, Right: wire-frame rendering

4.3   Paper Projection

A mobile screen using a paper works as a pinhole window into the 3D scene to provide a user with additional information. Just as if the user were actually in the 3D scene, the user can move the paper to an arbitrary position and orientation, thereby obtaining additional information about the projected 3D models on the tabletop screen, such as a cross-sectional image or an alternative rendering (see Figure 3).

These techniques are very useful for architectural tasks. Architects often need to investigate cross-sectional images on arbitrary planes from a variety of viewpoints. However, it is difficult to define plane equations and viewpoints in 3D CAD software. With the proposed system, the user can specify a plane equation and a viewpoint easily and naturally. As the paper has no specific devices attached, such as tracking IR markers, any size and shape of paper for the mobile pinhole window is available. A plane equation of the paper is calculated using its depth data, namely the distances between the paper surface and the Kinect camera. A bounding box is set in advance, enabling the Kinect to ignore areas outside the box, and obtain depth information about the real objects inside the bounding box. Then, the plane equation of the paper is fixed by applying the least square method to point clouds inside the bounding box. To eliminate the user's hand and specify the equation more precisely, points whose distance from the result of the least-squares method exceeds a threshold are eliminated, and the remaining points are processed by the least-squares method again. After iterating this process several times (twice or three times are usually sufficient), we obtain an accurate paper equation. Besides, to avoid overlapping display on the table-top projection from the paper projection, the region outside the projection of the paper should be black. We prepared a binary image to project exclusively on the object's surface inside the bounding box (see Figure 4, (b)) and then, we subtract the black part in the binary image from the paper projection (see Figure 4).

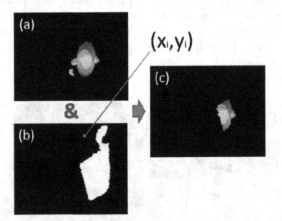

Fig. 4. (a):a paper projection before computing (b):a binary image of the objects above the surface (c):a result image by subtract (b) from (a)

4.4   Interaction Using Mobile Paper

A couple of interaction techniques using the mobile paper have been implemented at the moment. When a user conducting architecture design tasks uses the paper to obtain additional information, he/she performs manipulations to a 3D model so that the paper projection shows its detailed information. Figure 5 shows example interaction techniques implemented in this system ('pick up' and 'release'). These techniques enable the user to manipulate a 3D model such as rotation and translation by tilting and moving the paper, respectively. Even though the user can only rotate the 3D model while the paper's equation remains detectable (if the paper is vertical to the Kinect camera, for example, its plane equation is not computable), in many cases the user can conduct manipulation tasks using the paper.

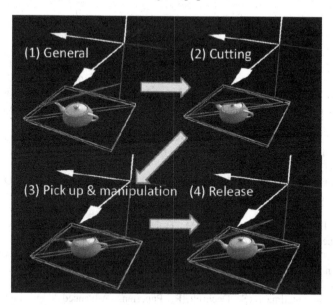

Fig. 5. Interaction using the mobile paper: the 3D model is synchronized with the movement of the paper by picking up mode

5   Future Work and Conclusion

In this paper we present an interactive interface that integrates a tabletop platform with mobile paper projection. The paper projection works as a pinhole window to show additional information and to enable a user to manipulate a 3D model intuitively and naturally.

As it is an ongoing work, many issues remain to be investigated. In architecture design tasks, there are several situations, for example, a designer solely explores his plan by manipulating an architectural model, a designer and developers discuss about construction processes using the model, a designer explains about his plan by showing details of the model, and so on. To extend the system for multiple users, it needs to conduct multi-user head tracking. Also the current tabletop projection may have to be changed to a normal projection so that all the users can see the same image or switched between individual users' correct-perspective projection. Using multiple papers for 3D model manipulation and projection by individual users is not within the scope of our implementation plan, because the need for such functions in architecture design tasks is not clear at the moment. Using a flexible paper as proposed in [9] to show cross-sectional images may make our application scenarios more convincing. We plan to ask professional architectural designers for intensive user studies to evaluate the system.

Acknowledgement. This work has been supported by JSPS Kakenhi Grant Number 25282048.

References

1. Kinect for Windows, http://www.microsoft.com/en-us/kinectforwindows/
2. Benko, H., Jota, R., Wilson, A.: Miragetable: Freehand Interaction on a Projected Augmented Reality Tabletop. In: Proc. of CHI 2012, Austin, TX, pp. 199–208 (2012)
3. Benko, H., Wilson, A.D.: DepthTouch: Using Depth-Sensing Camera to Enable Freehand Interactions On and Above the Interactive Surface, Microsoft Technical Report, MSR-TR-2009-23 (2009)
4. Hilliges, O., Izadi, S., Wilson, A.D., Hodges, S., Garcia-Mendoza, A., Butz, A.: Interactions in the Air: Adding Further Depth to Interactive Tabletops. In: Proc. of UIST 2009, Victoria, Canada, pp. 139–148 (2009)
5. Hilliges, O., Kim, D., Izadi, S., Weiss, M., Wilson, A.: Holodesk: Direct 3D Interactions with a Situated See-through Display. In: Proc. of CHI 2012, Austin, TX, pp. 2421–2430 (2012)
6. Holman, D., Vertegaal, R., Altosaar, M., Troje, N., Johns, D.: Paper Windows: Interaction Techniques for Digital Paper. In: Proc. of CHI 2005, Portland, OR, pp. 591–599 (2005)
7. Spindler, M., Büschel, W., Dachselt, R.: Use Your Head: Tangible Windows for 3D Information Spaces in a Tabletop Environment. In: Proc. of ITS 2012, Cambridge, MA, pp. 245–254 (2012)
8. Spindler, M., Stellmach, S., Dachselt, R.: Paperlens: Advanced Magic Lens Interaction above the Tabletop. In: Proc. of ITS 2009, Banff, Canada, pp. 69–76 (2009)
9. Steimle, J., Jordt, A., Maes, P.: Flexpad: Highly Flexible Bending Interactions for Projected Handheld Displays. In: Proc. of CHI 2013, Paris, France, pp. 237–246 (2013)
10. Ware, C., Arthur, K., Booth, K.S.: Fish Tank Virtual Reality. In: Proc. of CHI 1993, Amsterdam, Netherlands, pp. 37–42 (1993)
11. Wilson, A.D.: Depth-Sensing Video Cameras for 3D. In: Proc. of ITS 2007, Newport, RI, pp. 201–204 (2007)
12. Wilson, A.D., Benko, H.: Combining Multiple Depth Cameras and Projectors for Interactions on, above and between Surfaces. In: Proc. of UIST 2010, New York, NY, pp. 273–282 (2010)
13. Zhang, Z.: A Flexible New Technique for Camera Calibration. IEEE Transactions on Pattern Analysis and Machine Intelligence 22(11), 1330–1334 (2000)

Creating Interactive Flexible Surfaces
with Origami Tessellations

Kentaro Go, Yuichiro Kinoshita, Kohei Kaneko, and Reiji Kozono

University of Yamanashi, 4-3-11 Takeda, Kofu 400-8511, Japan
{go,ykinoshita}@yamanashi.ac.jp,
{kohei.kaneko,reiji.kozono}@ttmuh.org

Abstract. A device concept featuring interactive flexible surfaces with origami tessellations is presented. The Origami Tessellation Display (OTD) enables users to dynamically transform the shape of interactive surfaces from flat to three-dimensionally curved surfaces. We explore the design space of such devices by investigating different types, forms, and sizes. Furthermore, we propose a set of interaction principles and techniques based on the physical form of the OTD. A brief discussion of a user-based deformation study using low-fidelity prototypes as part of the user-centered design process is also presented.

Keywords: Tangible interaction, mobile devices, origami tessellations, foldable displays, flexible displays, folding, input and output devices.

1   Introduction

Flexible interactive surfaces have received continuous attention in the human-computer interaction community [7]. Researchers have been engaged in creating flexible display devices in addition to designing interactive gestures for command input. Furthermore, emerging technologies such as electronic paper, full color high-resolution flexible Organic Light-Emitting Diode (OLED) displays, and real-time tracking and mobile projection technology provide new opportunities to investigate deformable interactive displays.

Recent studies have focused on exploring different input and output techniques including user-based deformation [8, 12] and device-controlled deformation [7, 13, 15]. These techniques are affected and afforded by materials and the design of their surfaces. Several user-based deformation studies have developed prototypes and mock-ups to investigate specific user gestures [8, 12]. However, further investigation of new materials and designs to create novel interactive surfaces is required.

In this study, we propose the concept of Origami Tessellation Display (OTD), an interactive flexible surface with origami tessellations (Fig. 1). The primary goal of this study is to explore the design space around OTDs based on their physical forms, properties, and restrictions. We are particularly interested in exploring some unique capabilities of origami tessellation as an interactive flexible surface because this domain presents a range of opportunities.

T. Yuizono et al. (Eds.): CollabTech 2014, CCIS 460, pp. 119–126, 2014.

Fig. 1. Origami tessellation display prototypes

2   Related Work

The development of OTDs has been inspired by industrial applications of origami in addition to deformable and shape displays. Herein we briefly summarize previous studies in these areas.

2.1   Industrial Application of Origami

Origami is the Japanese art of paper folding. It has been applied to the design of a variety of products from lampshades to large space structures [14]. Mitani developed a series of design methods for a three-dimensional origami base [14], which allows designers to create gift boxes and lampshades. Tachi explored rigid-foldable thick origami in which thick materials, such as boards and panels, are connected with hinges to allow architects to create foldable three-dimensional designs [14]. Perhaps, the most famous industrial application of origami is Miura-ori, designed to package a large membrane in space. A common structure observed in these industrial applications includes repeating patterns of specific shapes. These repeating patterns are referred to as tessellations [2].

2.2   Deformable Displays

Many researchers have focused on gestures for deformation-based input modality for flexible displays; two basic gestures are bending and folding. Gummi [16] is a deformable handheld computing device, which provides a set of interaction techniques that leverage bending as an input technique to manipulate digital content. Twnd [5] and Bookisheet [3] have also introduced bend gestures to issue commands. Paper-Phone [10] and PaperWindow [6] introduced basic gestures for digital papers that involve bending as a key gesture.

Folding is another basic gesture for deformable displays. Lee et al. [11] demonstrated four different types of foldable and resizable displays. Foldable user interfaces [3] leverage cardboard that can be bent and folded to manipulate a three-dimensional GUI.

Finally, a series of user-generated gestures for deformable displays has been investigated. Lee et al. [12] elicited gestures for a set of basic commands performed with imaginary flexible displays composed of plastic, paper, and cloth. Similarly, Khalil-beigi et al. [8] investigated a physical design space for folding gestures and a set of novel interaction techniques to propose double-sided foldable displays.

2.3   Shape Displays

Shape displays, also known as actuatable displays, physically move display surface components. Many shape displays have been proposed, including Lumen [15], FEELEX [7], and Relief display [13]. In these projects, physical movements on a surface are created with actuators. Additionally, sensors are implemented in actuation rods to behave as input devices.

3   The Origami Tessellation Display Concept

In this section, we investigate the design space of OTDs, which are based on origami tessellation models.

3.1   Origami Tessellation

A tessellation is a collection of repeating patterns of specific shapes, in which the pattern fills a plane with no gaps or overlaps. In origami tessellation, pleats are used to connect basic shapes; typically, a folded model is created from a sheet of paper.

We use Water Bomb tessellation [4] as an example to explain our OTD concept. Fig. 2(a) shows a crease pattern, and Fig. 2(b) shows a folded model of the Water Bomb tessellation. A folded Water Bomb tessellation model has two states: flat and hemisphere. In the flat state, the model has a flat surface that is tiled with square bases. In the hemisphere state, the model achieves a three-dimensional surface that is both pliant and curved. Furthermore, it has slits (pleats), folded edges, and corners surrounding a square base. These visible elements can allow users to touch, trace, and point. As the slits open, the size of the visualization and interaction surface increases. This seamless transition between the flat and hemisphere states provides new capabilities for deformable interactive surfaces.

3.2   Interaction Styles

Our OTD interaction grammar was motivated by the natural manipulation of paper and foldable displays. A set of potential gestures for OTDs may include hold, flip, flex, twist, rub, touch, point, and trace gestures. These gestures are affected and afforded by the physical form of the OTD.

For example, in touch and point gestures, the OTD allows users to touch the top of a square unit or the sides of a slit area, and to point the corners of a square unit. Similarly, in a trace gesture, users can trace the edges of a folded pattern. The edges surrounding a square base are candidates for circular tracing. Another candidate for circular tracing may be connecting edges that look like a star with four corners. This is a unique capability of the OTD.

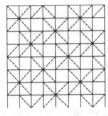 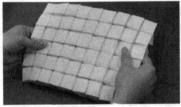 

(a) Example of   (b) Folded models: flat state (left) and hemisphere state (right)
crease pattern

Fig. 2. Water Bomb tessellation as an origami tessellation display prototype

3.3   Input vs. Output Devices

Our OTD can be used as an input device, output device, and as an input/output device simultaneously. As an input device, users can conduct user-based deformation using the various interaction styles described in the previous section. As an output device, the OTD can be implemented as a shape display with actuators. In origami tessellations, basic units are connected by pleats; thus, actuators can be attached to the outside edges to provide an overall form change. Finally, an input/output device can have potentials of both the input and output methods discussed so far, which may be suitable for implementing interactive deformable displays.

3.4   Device and Unit Sizes

Design decisions for device and unit sizes must be considered when creating an OTD. A specific size of the overall shape offers different characteristics. For example, an A4-sized OTD can be easily held with two hands and interacted with using two-handed gestures such as flex and twist. OTDs with sizes smaller than A4 are appropriate for a mobile setting and may be suitable for interactive surfaces for user-based deformation. In contrast, a large table-sized OTD may be appropriate for mounting in a room or public spaces and may be suitable for interactive surfaces for device-controlled deformation.

Another aspect to consider in OTDs is the size of the basic unit. For example, in the Water Bomb tessellation, designers must consider the size of the square units. A large square unit suggests that the folded model has a large pleat and deep slit. The effective resolution of the OTD depends on each unit size and the number of units.

3.5   Conceivable Implementation Technologies

A key design decision to be considered is the type of technology that will be employed for a display unit. This decision is influenced by the factors discussed so far. Specifically, either input, output or both, as well as unit sizes are the issue. Generally, a paper-folded tessellation model combined with a projector and camera is the standard approach. To increase brightness, a tiny unit with a full color LED can be an alternative. Another approach is to use a small OLED screen as a basic unit, which provides a similar profile to the Tilt Display [1] proposed by Alexander et al. Note that our OTD has pleats as the interactive surface; therefore, a hybrid approach may be employed in which an OLED screen is used as a basic unit and projector screen or LED as pleats.

3.6 Application Examples

The concept of the OTD can be applied to numerous examples. In the following, we will describe three major examples that we are currently working on. The examples include an interactive street map, deformable toolglass and magic lenses, and personal and shared information control on an interactive table.

Interactive Street Maps. Displaying interactive street maps is a typical example for our OTD concept (Fig. 3(a)). In the flat state, the top flat surface, a tiled collection of square units, is used as a conventional interactive display. Users can issue traditional GUI commands with touch gestures as if it were a standard touch screen.

In contrast, in the hemisphere state, the overall shape of the display is not flat and slits become open and visible. The curved surface may be suitable for displaying a relatively large landscape. In this state, slits can be used as a new display layer for geographical information including climate, natural resource, and traffic information. In addition, the slit area can be used to interact with such information. As the slits open, a larger visualization and interaction surface is obtained. This seamless transition between flat and hemisphere states provides new capabilities for interactive street maps. Kinoshita et al. [9] discuss further use cases of interactive street maps on OTDs.

(a) Interactive Street Map

(b) Deformable toolglass and magic lenses

Fig. 3. Application examples for origami tessellation display

Deformable Toolglass and Magic Lenses. The concept of toolglass and magic lenses was proposed by Bier et al. [2]. The concept can be implemented using OTDs. Fig. 3(b) shows a schematic view of a toolglass and magic lenses using an OTD. Users operate see-through OTDs to visualize a preview and apply its effect to an object. Using the characteristics of the deformable display, some commands can be assigned to gestures such as flex, twist, and rub.

Personal and Shared Information Control on an Interactive Table. Supporting fluid transitions between group and personal work around a multi-user interactive tabletop is an important issue in co-located groupware. Our OTD concept can be applied to deal with this issue. Fig. 4 shows a table-sized OTD. In the flat state, the flat table top comprising square units is a shared public space. In the hemisphere state, the central part of the display moves upward to create a natural curved tabletop. Some slits and the area in front of a user are not visible by other collaborators, which create a personal user workspace.

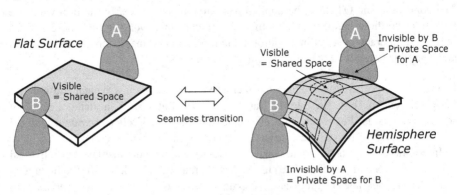

Fig. 4. Personal and shared information control on an interactive table

4   Proof-Of-Concept Prototype

To investigate different types of interactive gestures and their use cases further, we have constructed several paper prototypes. These prototypes incorporate the main physical properties of our display concept: lightweight, rigid, and easily handled. Fig. 1 shows prototypes for a user-based deformation study. Eighteen graduate and undergraduate students (fifteen males and three females) participated in this study.

The study consisted of four parts: prototype demonstration, user-based gesture generation, semi-structured interviews, and group discussions. We gathered the participants' background information, explained the primary goal of the study, and demonstrated a range of applications with the OTD. We then conducted a user-based gesture generation session. After the session, we conducted semi-structured interviews with the participants following a series of open-ended questions. Finally, we split the participants into four groups and asked them to engage in open discussion and brainstorming regarding commands, generated gestures, and further applications of and use cases for the OTD.

This user study found that participants were positive about OTDs and were enthusiastic about their practical applications. Some of the results are shown below. For further quantitative results from our prototype study, refer to Kinoshita et al. [9].

Partial list of OTD application ideas produced by the participants:

- *3D puzzle game*
- *3D video phone with slits as eye and mouth movement*
- *Reversi game*
- *Flexible cap displaying his/her brain map*

5   Conclusion

In this paper, we explored the origami tessellation display (OTD) concept by investigating the OTD design space based on physical form, properties, and restrictions. OTDs allow users to manipulate interactive surfaces in flat and three-dimensional states, and further allow seamless transition of the interaction mode. We discussed the properties of an OTD using Water Bomb tessellation as an example.

Future studies will include further research on types of tessellation other than Water Bomb to understand issues of the OTD concept and the examination of application examples to assess additional opportunities for OTDs.

Acknowledgements. This research was partially supported by the Ministry of Education, Culture, Sports, Science and Technology, Grant-in-Aid for Scientific Research (C) 24500144 and 23500160.

References

1. Alexander, J., Lucero, A., Subramanian, S.: Tilt display demonstration: a display surface with multi-axis tilt & actuation. In: Proc. MobileHCI 2012, pp. 213–214. ACM Press (2012)
2. Bier, E.A., Stone, M.C., Pier, K., Buxton, W., DeRose, T.D.: Toolglass and magic lenses: the see-through interface. In: Proc. SIGGRAPH 1993, pp. 73–80. ACM Press (1993)
3. Gallant, D.T., Seniuk, A.G., Vertegaal, R.: Towards more paper-like input: fexible input devices for foldable interaction styles. In: Proc. UIST 2008, pp. 283–286. ACM Press (2008)
4. Gjerde, E.: Origami tessellations: awe-inspiring geometric designs. A K Peters (2009)
5. Herkenrath, G., Karrer, T., Borchers, J.: Twend: twisting and bending as new interaction gesture in mobile devices. In: Ext. Abstracts CHI, pp. 3819–3824. ACM Press (2008)
6. Holman, D., Vertegaal, R., Altosaar, M.: PaperWindows: Interaction Techniques for Digital Paper. In: Proc. CHI 2005, pp. 591–599. ACM Press (2005)
7. Ishii, H., Lakatos, D., Bonanni, L., Labrune, J.B.: Radical atoms: beyond tangible bits, toward transformable materials. Interactions 19(1), 38–51 (2012)
8. Iwata, H., Yano, H., Nakaizumi, F., Kawamura, R.: Project FEELEX: Adding haptic surface to graphics. In: Proc. SIGRAPH 2001, pp. 469–476. ACM Press (2001)
9. Khalilbeigi, M., Lissermann, R., Kleine, W., Steimle, J.: FoldMe: interacting with double-sided foldable displays. In: Proc. TEI 2012, pp. 33–40. ACM Press (2012)
10. Kinoshita, Y., Go, K., Kozono, R., Kaneko, K.: Origami tessellation display: interaction techniques using origami-based deformable surfaces. In: Proc. CHI EA 2014, pp. 1837–1842. ACM Press (2014)

11. Lahey, B., Girouard, A., Burleson, W., Vertegaal, R.: PaperPhone: understanding the use of bend gestures in mobile devices with flexible electronic paper displays. In: Proc. CHI 2011, pp. 1303–1312. ACM Press (2011)

12. Lee, J.C., Hudson, S.E., Tse, E.: Foldable interactive displays. In: Proc. UIST 2008, pp. 287–290. ACM Press (2008)

13. Lee, S., Kim, S., Jim, B., Choi, E., Kim, B., Jia, X., Kim, D., Lee, K.: How users manipulate deformable display as input devices. In: Proc. CHI 2010, pp. 1647–1656. ACM Press (2010)

14. Leithinger, D., Ishii, H.: Relief: a scalable actuated shape display. In: Proc. TEI 2010, pp. 221–222. ACM Press (2010)

15. Nojima, T., Hagiwara, I.: Geometrical mathematics for origami and its industrial application. Kyoritsu Pub. (2012) (in Japanese)

16. Poupyrev, I., Nashida, T., Maruyama, S., Rekimoto, J., Yamaji, Y.: Lumen: Interactive visual and shape display for calm computing. In: ACM SIGGRAPH 2004 Emerging Technologies, 17 p. ACM Press (2004)

17. Schwesig, C., Poupyrev, I., Mori, E.: Gummi: User Interface for Deformable Computers. In: Proc. CHI 2003, pp. 954–955. ACM Press (2003)

Multilevel Analysis of Collaborative Activities Based on a Mobile Learning Scenario for Real Classrooms

Irene-Angelica Chounta[1], Adam Giemza[2], and Heinz Ulrich Hoppe[2]

[1] HCI Group, University of Patras, Greece
houren@upatras.gr
[2] Collide, University of Duisburg-Essen, Germany
{giemza,hoppe}@collide.info

Abstract. This paper describes the analysis of collaborative mobile learning activities. We explore the use of learning analytics for the evaluation of the performance of students as individuals and the performance of teams. We argue that traditional metrics used for learning analytics can provide insight with respect to the quality of the activity and the learning outcome. We propose a way to integrate innovative mobile learning scenarios into traditional classrooms and to analyze collaborative learning activities on both the group and the individual level.

Keywords: learning analytics, group activity, mobile learning, collaboration.

1 Introduction

During the past years, the idea of mobile phones as small computers empowering students to learn at any time and any place has been implemented in many educational scenarios. The variety of mobile learning scenarios ranges from applications inside the classroom, e.g., collaborative problem solving [1] and discussion tools [2], applications for field trips, e.g., language learning applications in the field [3] and data collecting applications [4, 5], or workplace learning scenarios [6] and educational (serious) games [7]. Mobile devices have a central role in these mobile learning activities.

Even though the use of mobile scenarios for learning activities is widely studied, the analysis of such activities is usually carried out through qualitative methods making it a tiresome and time consuming task [8, 9]. The analysis becomes more complicated when the mobile scenario aims to support collaborative activities. In order to support the task of analysis, researchers propose the use of learning analytics into a mobile learning context [10]. The advantage of mobile devices for learning analytics in comparison to classical desktop systems is that can they provide more information about the context of the user and his learning situation through the device's sensors.

It is argued that "*the term learning analytics is currently mobilized within a multi-disciplinary community of researchers*" [11], thus offering new possibilities and setting new research goals and questions. In this paper we explore the use of a mobile

T. Yuizono et al. (Eds.): CollabTech 2014, CCIS 460, pp. 127–142, 2014.
© Springer-Verlag Berlin Heidelberg 2014

learning scenario for assembling computers in a traditional school classroom. The scenario is designed for computer science classes and teaches the functionality of a computer by relating the theoretical concepts to real-world technology with hands-on experience. The students are guided through a scenario using the Mobilogue app on a smartphone. The scenario involves scanning QR codes attached to computer parts, reading background information, watching instructional videos and assembling the computer step by step. For the analysis of the activity we use learning analytics that derive from the activity logfiles and transcripts of the activity recorded by experts. The learning outcome was evaluated by knowledge tests and questionnaires were used to evaluate students' experience.

2   Related Work

User data is a valuable source of information for the analysis of collaborative activities in the fields of CSCL and CSCW. Researchers use data-driven, bottom up approaches to define metrics of user activity. These metrics are usually studied for potential correlations to the quality of collaboration or to the quality of the outcome. The number of messages exchanged in a dialogue or the average number of words per message are typical metrics for the assessment of collaborative practice [12, 13]. For the case of shared workspaces, the use of metrics that represent the symmetry of user activity is common to evaluate coordination [14, 15]. Depending on the learning context, activity metrics may vary. Metrics deriving from graph theory, such as density, have been proposed to assess collaboration quality [16] while metrics of spatial proximity have been proposed for scenarios such like jigsaw puzzles or algorithmic flowcharts [18]. Significant part of the literature is dedicated to the use of time-related metrics such as total duration of an activity, time gaps or time proximity [17, 18, 19]. Apart from the evaluation of typical collaborative learning scenarios, activity metrics have been proposed to support communities of practice [20] or to analyze the activity of users involved in location-based games [21, 22]. Mobile learning, in particular, constitutes a suitable field for the adaptation of data analysis methods deriving from multidisciplinary fields such as CSCL and EDM [10].

A combination of assembling a computer with mobile support has been presented in [23]. The focus of this work was to link user created (tutorial) videos with environmental objects and to provide the combined information for others as video support upon scanning tagged objects. This system was evaluated with students who were assigned four different computer assembly tasks. The tasks involved the creation of videos linked with the RFID marked objects. The result provided content to a second group of learners that had to fulfill the same tasks with support through the LORAMS system, which served the user created videos. In contrast to that, our scenario focuses on the guided support of the assembly task and the consumption of learning content. The guidance follows a strict path through the task and instructs the learner part by part. The relevant information and video instructions are provided based on the QR-code attached to the computer part. Additionally, students can capture videos and images of their activities using the Mobilogue app. However, these artifacts are not incorporated into the scenario directly, but can be later reused for reporting on the field trip and follow-up activities with the teacher. Hsu et al. [24] propose a situated multimedia ubiquitous learning (SMUL) system that applies mobile devices in a computer assembly learning activity. The system supports learners by providing information for the assembly task by scanning RFID (radio frequency identification) tags on the computer hardware components. The study shows that the context-aware ubiquitous learning approach achieved better learning effects compared to conventional approaches. Our study also aims to demonstrate the flexibility of the Mobilogue framework as a general tool to design, set up and orchestrate station-based learning scenarios with mobile support used for the Computer Kit scenario. Instead of RFID tags, Mobilogue produces QR codes for identifying learning stations, in this case computer parts that are cheap and easy to create for schools and learners. Furthermore the application does not demand specialized hardware (like NFC or RFID readers in smartphones) but only relies on a camera, which allows students to user their own devices.

3   Mobilogue Computer Kit

3.1   The Scenario "Computer Kit"

Technology is more and more in the focus of everyday life with the rapidly increasing use of digital devices like smartphones, tablets, computers and gaming consoles. While their usage becomes very natural, resulting in an implicit awareness of technology, the knowledge about its basic functionality often does not matter. However, the knowledge of computer architecture and the curiosity about technology are very important as STEM education becomes a crucial issue [25] all over the world. Especially computer science is very important for future generations with the high impact of technology in all areas nowadays.

Fig. 1. Initial setting of the Computer Kit scenario

The curriculum for high school level students in Germany includes teaching the structure and functioning of a computer (i.e., Von Neumann architecture). In order to support teachers to communicate this fundamental topic, we designed a scenario using our Mobilogue framework [26]. The scenario teaches hands-on the theoretical concepts in combination with real-world technology. Students use a smartphone as a guide for assembling a computer while they receive background information about the computer parts, their functionality and video-based support on how to install them. Fig.1 shows the initial setting of the Computer Kit scenario. The students are equipped with a smartphone running the Mobilogue app and all computer hardware components with accompanied by QR codes. Fig. 4a shows the Mobilogue Android app with an information page about the computer mainboard. Students walk through the scenario step by step until they have fully assembled the computer and start it up to check their success.

3.2   The Mobilogue Framework

Mobilogue [26] is a flexible tool for authoring and conducting mobile learning field trip scenarios. It maps the concept of field trips onto guided tours across multiple (physical) locations supported by a mobile device. Its basic pedagogical underpinning is learning at stations (or learning circles). The learning takes place at stations, i.e. specific locations, by providing content related to the place or an object at that place and additional stimuli to foster interaction and curiosity by challenging the learner with a quiz. Locations can be spatially distributed around an area or – like in the Computer Kit case – simply represented by physical objects. These locations can also be interpreted as stations of a tour in a certain order. Mobilogue guides the learner across the different stations of the tour, i.e., the learning scenario.

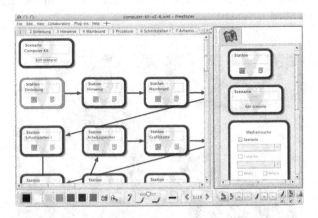

Fig. 2. Graph-based Mobilogue authoring environment with Computer Kit scenario

Mobilogue consists of four elements: the authoring environment to create mobile guidance scenarios, the backend containing the repository for storage and exchange as well as the action logging service to store user activity logs, the mobile application for running the authored scenarios and finally the Mobilogue portal for management and supervision (Fig. 3). The authoring environment enables teachers as well as students to create field trip scenarios without the need to learn a complex authoring tool or to care about the technological background. The basic concept of the authoring environment is related to consuming (multimedia) content in different locations in a certain (guided) order. The authoring tool (Fig. 2) allows to create such locations and to organize them in a certain sequence as the guided field trip for the learner through different locations. The authoring workflow is implemented as a plug-in of the graph-based modeling environment FreeStyler [27]. The modeled workflow graph is later interpreted as the route along the scenario on the mobile devices.

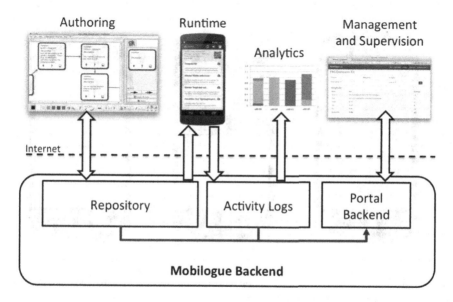

Fig. 3. Mobilogue architecture overview

The Mobilogue backend includes the repository as the mediator between the authoring environment and the Mobilogue app. The authoring environment publishes scenarios to the repository and makes them thereby available to the mobile application. The Android application on the other hand retrieves scenarios via a web service from the repository and stores them in the local database on the phone for offline access. All user activities are logged on the mobile devices and locally persisted in case of no Internet access. In the case of connectivity to the Mobilogue backend, it sends all user logs to the activity log service. The log service provides web services for storing and retrieving action logs in JSON Activity Streams format[1]. We will present later how we use this web service for extracting the relevant log data. The last

---

[1] JSON Activity Streams format specification 1.0 - http://activitystrea.ms/ (last visited: April 2014).

part of the backend is the portal backend component. It servers the Mobilogue portal where scenario authors can manage their uploaded scenarios, teachers or tutors can create and organize groups for classroom runs and finally users can review their Mobilogue runs. We will not further describe this component as it is not subject to this study.

The Mobilogue app acts as the runtime for Mobilogue scenarios. Scenarios are retrieved from the repository and run by the native Android application. The app renders the scenario as information pages with images and text (Fig. 4a), as multiple choice or free text quiz, provides awareness about the performance and progress of the user (Fig. 4c) and also plays multimedia data like video (Fig. 4b), sound and HTML-based content packages.

Fig. 4. Mobilogue app with (a) information screen about mainboards (b) instructional video how to install a CPU (c) progress review screen

The app uses the built-in camera to scan QR codes and to decode the identifier of the learning station. The scanned station is queried from the locally cached scenario and the appropriate information is presented. During a scenario run, the user performs multiple activities: starting a scenario run, scanning a (valid) code, visiting an information page, answering a quiz, watching a video, etc. When the user finishes the scenario, he/she also finishes the run. All the user actions are logged to the activity logs service in JSON Activity Streams format.

The following extract exemplifies the format: It contains the date of occurrence (*published*), the *actor* of the activity (in Mobilogue an anonymized run id), the *verb* describing the activity (in this case a visit of the *object*, i.e., a location identified through the id). Based on this information, we can identify all actions of a user through the persistent run id (throughout one scenario run). The detailed information of the location can be queried from the scenario document based on the logged location id.

```
{
  "published" : ISODate("2014-02-27T07:22:38.373Z"),
  "actor" : {
    "id" : "ac86989c-2ca6-408a-b86a-694873f1c79b",
    "objectType" : "run"
  },
  "verb" : "visit",
  "object" : {
    "id" : "05ae5db61e83b761:7aa20533:13f38bfb685:-7fbb",
    "objectType" : "location"
  }
}
```

A complete scenario run produces a sequence of activity objects, the activity stream. The action logs service allows querying such a stream for single runs, for a certain scenario, for a certain timeframe, etc. Consequently, we are able to use these data for the analysis of the activity.

4   Method of the Study

In this paper we analyze the activity of groups of students who work together in order to assemble a PC. The study was carried out in two phases. In the first phase we conducted a preliminary study (Case A). The results were used to improve the study set up and a second study (Case B) followed shortly after.

In both studies each group was supported by one mobile device that walked them through the process according to the Mobilogue scenario "Computer Kit". We provided each team with one mobile device in order to ensure that the students who formed a team would collaborate and work together towards the common goal. Moreover our aim was to record the strategy of each team with respect to roles' adaptation and whether this strategy would affect its practice. We argue that members of homogeneous teams (teams that consist of students of similar knowledge background) will get involved in all the stages and roles of the activity. On the other hand, members of heterogeneous teams (i.e. students of different knowledge background who co-exist in the same team) will follow a certain plan with discrete roles and they will stick to that plan throughout the activity.

To that end, each group was given the freedom to plan its practice and make important decisions (e.g. which group member would operate the device, whether they would switch roles in turns, etc). The practice of teams was further studied with respect to the teams' homogeneity. To analyze the activity, we used the logfiles of the Mobilogue application to extract activity metrics. We argue that these metrics reflect the activity on a group level since the operator of the device does not act on his own, but follows the instructions of the group. Due to the strictly controlled scenario, activity metrics such as total number of QR-code scans or total number of actions cannot be used. Therefore we explore the use of time-related metrics such average time gap among consequent actions (avg_timegap) and average response time to quizzes (avg_resp). The time gap is measured as the time between two "page visits", i.e., the time between opening an information page and opening the succeeding page in the mobile app. The time gaps differ regarding the content. Some short information texts can be grasped quickly, whereas the tutorial videos take up to 50 seconds. Time is a key factor for collaborative activities [28] and time related metrics have been used to assess collaboration quality. For example, average response time in chat has been found to correlate negatively with collaboration quality [14]. This indicates that groups who collaborate efficiently are faster in their responses. The average time gap among consequent actions is an indication of the rhythm (or speed) of group activity. Groups that coordinate efficiently are expected to work on a faster pace and therefore demonstrate smaller time gaps between consequent actions. The score, as computed from the quizzes of the Mobilogue scenario, was also introduced as a metric of group activity. In Case B, two evaluators were asked to monitor the activity and take notes with respect to students practice (activity transcripts). The transcripts were further used to provide insight into the group dynamics.

In order to measure the learning impact of the application of the Mobilogue scenario, the students were asked to take pre and post knowledge tests. Each test consisted of ten questions relevant to the learning activity. In addition, the students filled in questionnaires regarding their experience. In Case A the questionnaires were used for the evaluation of the Mobilogue application while in Case B we used questionnaires for the evaluation of the collaborative aspect of the activity itself and the students' experience.

5   Results

In the following paragraphs we present the results of the two case studies, Case A and Case B. Overall, the purpose of the study was to explore the use of learning analytics in a mobile learning scenario. Therefore, we analyze the practice of teams with respect to the logfiles of the application that mediated the activity and in combination with the learning outcome, as evaluated by knowledge tests and observations made by experts during the realization of the activity.

5.1   Case Study A

The first case study took place during a school computer course. Seventeen (17) students, aged from 13 to 15, participated in total. The students were randomly grouped in five teams. The whole duration of the activity was about one hour and a half. One mobile device was given to each team (Fig. 1). There was no instruction on how to use it (in turns, randomly etc) other than to follow the Mobilogue scenario. The students were advised by the teacher to document their activities for later reflections (Fig. 5a). Fig. 5a gives an impression on how the students followed the tutorial videos in order to assembly the computer part.

The results of the case study are portrayed in Table 1. Regarding the profiles of the teams as assessed by the pretest, the results portray a team with good knowledge of the learning field (team A), both on a group and on an individual level (average group score = 6.25, maximum individual score = 8), a weak team (team E) on group and individual level scores (average group score = 1, maximum individual score = 1) while the rest three teams were of average performance. After the ending of the activity, the students took a posttest. The results show that teams of average performance in the pretest achieved the greatest improvement, both on average as well as on the individual level. The "good" team (team A) maintained the same score on average and scored less on the individual level while the "bad" team (team E) slightly improved but overall its performance was still low. The scores of the knowledge test were also reflected in the quiz score. Team A scored the highest while team E scored the lowest.

The average response time (avg_resp) does not follow a certain pattern with respect to either the score of the quiz or the knowledge tests. On the other hand, the average time gap (avg_timegap) correlates negatively with the quiz score. Teams that have a high quiz score are also faster throughout the activity. This also shows that teams with good pre-knowledge tend to move faster through the activity.

Fig. 5. (a) Students taking pictures to document their run (b) students watching video instructions on how to install RAM

Table 1. Case Study A: Results of pre and post knowledge tests and activity metrics as computed from the logfiles of the Mobilogue application

| | Pretest Scores | | Posttest Scores | | | | |
	avg_group	max_idv	avg_group	max_idv	avg_time gap (sec)	avg_resp (sec)	Quiz Score
teamA	6.25	8	6.25	7	27.63	32.02	120
teamB	3.75	5	6.25	8	36.56	56.96	120
teamC	4.33	5	5.67	7	37.14	23.70	100
teamD	2.67	4	6.00	7	37.91	31.55	90
teamE	1.00	1	2.00	3	38.43	57.43	80

In order to measure team homogeneity, we compared the average group score (avg_group) to the maximum individual scores (max_idv) for each team. Team E, for example, scored the lowest score both in the knowledge test on a group and individual level therefore is homogeneous (avg_group – max_idv = 0). Team A, on the other hand, is the most heterogeneous team based on the test results (avg_group – max_idv = 1.75) with the rest of the teams falling in between. We should note that Team A had no knowledge gain according to the tests however, that can be justified since the highest score overall was already achieved by the same team. The comparison of pre and posttest scores shows that strongly heterogeneous teams increase their homogeneity and vice versa, with the exception of the weak team that showed no difference. Heterogeneous teams also portray smaller time gaps i.e. they follow the mobile scenario in a faster pace. This could indicate that in heterogeneous teams, the students who have prior knowledge or experience take the lead. However, in this case study there were no activity records or transcripts and therefore we cannot have a clear picture on group dynamics.

5.2   Case Study B

The original study (case A) was repeated in order to improve the experimental setup and to further validate the results. To that end, we asked from expert evaluators to attend the study and take notes of observations with respect to group dynamics. In particular, the experts were asked to observe the behavior of individuals within teams. In addition, the students were asked to keep notes of the role each individual chose to have within the team, if any, i.e. to operate the device, to take notes, to assemble the device. The learning effect was evaluated by pre and post knowledge tests. The students took those tests individually. Each test consisted of ten questions which were related to the learning objective. Overall, 24 students (13-15 years old) participated in the study. The students attended a computer school course and the teacher of the class gave a lecture prior to the study to ensure that all students would have the necessary background. The students were grouped into six teams of four. The grouping was done by the teacher with respect to the students' skills and general impression. The results for Case B are presented in Table 2.

Table 2. Case Study B: Results of pre and post knowledge tests and activity metrics as computed from the logfiles of the application

	Pretest Scores		Posttest Scores		avg_time gap (sec)	avg_resp (sec)	Quiz Score
	avg_group	max_idv	avg_group	max_idv			
team00	2	4	3.5	7	20.89	51.88	120
team 01	5.75	9	7.5	8	23.42	49.02	120
team 02	4.25	5	6	7	24.00	45.73	110
team 03	6.5	8	6.5	7	25.84	61.99	90
team 04	5.5	7	7.25	8	40.44	72.51	70
team 05	1	2	6	9	27.75	82.56	70

The six teams participating in Case B can be grouped into three categories with respect to their performance, as evaluated from the pretest scores: (a) weak (team00 and team05), (b) average (team01, team02, team04) (c) strong (team03). Two teams (team00 and team01) are strongly heterogeneous, regarding the difference among group and maximum individual score. Team02 is the most homogeneous, according to the same criterion. The grouping of the teams regarding homogeneity was also confirmed by the teacher.

The scores of the knowledge posttest indicate that students' performance improved on a group level (47% on average). The "strong" team (team03) was the only team with a zero knowledge gain while the maximum knowledge gain on a group level was scored by a "weak" team (team05). The score also improved for maximum, individual performance (31% on average) although there were two cases of "knowledge loss" (team01 and team 03). The quiz score does not correlate to either the pretest or the posttest score. The best scores were achieved by team00 and team01 which were perceived as "weak" and "medium" teams respectively. On the other hand, the "strong" team (team03) achieved a medium score in the quiz. That shows that the quiz score is not a good indicator of either pre-knowledge or learning outcome.

In order to measure group homogeneity, we compared the group and individual scores of the knowledge tests for each team, as in Case A. The comparison showed that weak learners forming heterogeneous teams or medium ability learners forming homogeneous teams do not necessarily achieve the maximum knowledge gain in the current learning setting, as expected [29]. For example, a homogeneous weak team that does not follow a strict role distribution but allows its members to get involved freely (team05) achieves a higher knowledge gain than a heterogeneous weak team where one, or more, experienced members take the lead and assign a strict role policy (team00). Even though the heterogeneous team scored higher in the activity quizzes, the performance of the individual members was not satisfactory on average and they were disappointed with respect to the activity, as the post-questionnaires reveal. This also led to the increase of the heterogeneity of the weak teams since there were students who took the lead and were more benefited than the group average. On the contrary, the average and strong groups became more homogeneous because the "good" students either appeared to have "knowledge loss" in the posttests or there was no room for big improvement in comparison to the group average.

The time-related activity metrics were also studied with respect to the learning outcome and quiz performance. The average time gap (avg_timegap) correlates negatively to the quiz score. This was also observed in Case A. Teams that moved faster in the scenario achieved higher quiz scores. Taking into consideration that the heterogeneous teams achieved higher scores (team00 and team01), this finding confirms the existence of a student (or more) who takes the leading role. This however does not ensure or presuppose the increase of knowledge gain on a group level.

The students were allowed to organize their practice freely and decide which member will undertake what role, to what extent, etc. In case B, the activity was monitored by the students who kept transcripts of their own work, as well as by experts who recorded the practice of the teams. We identified three roles that the students undertook throughout the scenario: a. the operator of the mobile device (operator), b. the one who was keeping notes (scriber) and c. the one who assembles the computer (assembler). Four out of six teams did not follow a strict policy in roles' distribution. All students undertook different roles as the activity progressed. Fig. 6 gives an overview of the roles' distribution per team member for all teams. Some teams adopted turn taking in their practice (team01) while others followed a seemingly unstructured way (team04). Two out of six teams (team00 and team03) followed a certain plan throughout the whole duration of the activity and their members maintained the same roles. This strategy was not effective for their overall performance and these teams portrayed the lowest knowledge gain on a group level. They claimed it was not easy to assemble the computer and learn about hardware while working in a group. There were also some negative comments regarding the practice of their fellow team members.

Table 3. Average ratings per team on the questionnaire used to evaluate the experience of students

	Q1	Q2	Q3	Q4
team00	3.5	4	3	0
team01	4	4	3.75	1
team02	3.25	3.5	3.75	0.75
team03	3.25	3	2.25	1.5
team04	3	4	3.25	0.75
team05	3.75	4	3.5	0

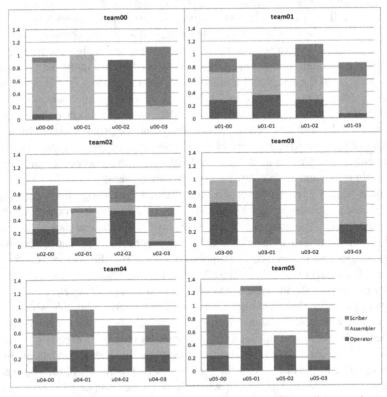

Fig. 6. Roles' distribution per team and among team members. Three discrete roles, with respect to users activity, were recorded: the scriber, the assembler and the operator. The figure presents the involvement of each student per role for the whole duration of the activity.

The students were also asked whether they would have been more efficient if they worked on their own. The good and average teams perceive that they would have done better on their own, while the weak teams (team00, team05) replied negatively. Overall the questionnaire regarding the students experience consisted of four questions. These questions were:

Q1: *"After the end of the activity I knew more about the structure of a computer".*

Q2: *"The activity was fun"*

Q3: *"It was easier to assemble the computer and learn about the hardware while working in a team"*

Q4: *"I could have done it better if I were working on my own"*

The results of the post-questionnaire are portrayed in Table 3.Each question was rated on a five-point Likert scale by all the team members, where zero (0) stands for "I do not agree" and four (4) stands for "I fully agree". The overall rating per team (team00 – team05) on each one of the four questions (Q1 – Q4) as presented in **Table 3**, was computed as the average of the ratings of the team members.

6   Conclusion

This paper presents the application of a mobile learning scenario in a traditional, collaborative classroom setting and the analysis of the activity. To that end, we carried out two case studies where students had to work together in groups with the support of a mobile device (smartphone) in order to assemble a computer. Our goal was to study the application of learning analytics for mobile learning activities on the group as well as on the individual level. The activity of each group was analyzed with the combined use of logfile analysis, activity transcripts, questionnaires and knowledge tests. We argue that the multilevel analysis can provide valuable information and enhance mobile learning.

The activities were analyzed with respect to the learning outcome as well as the practice of users. The analysis of the results revealed that the scenario application was more effective for students of weak and medium knowledge background. The knowledge gain in the case of teams of weak and medium performance was bigger and the students of such teams also perceived it as a helpful experience. On the contrary, strong teams showed little or no knowledge gain at all on a group level. On the individual level, students with high performance in the pretest, scored lower in the post knowledge tests while they noted they could have performed better if working on their own. The teams were also categorized as heterogeneous or homogeneous with respect to their members' individual performance. It was shown that heterogeneous teams achieved a higher score in the quizzes set by the scenario, although there was no correlation to the overall knowledge gain or overall score of the knowledge tests. The heterogeneous teams also moved faster through the stages of the scenario which points that the "stronger" members pushed forward the rest of the team. Overall, it was found that homogeneous teams tend to increase their heterogeneity and vice versa. This was expected since in heterogeneous teams the weakest members have more room for improvement that the strong ones. In homogeneous teams, some of the team members inevitably will benefit more than the rest, increasing the team's heterogeneity. Each team was allowed to choose its action plan (i.e. who would undertake what role etc.) as long as they would follow the instructions of the Mobilogue scenario. The majority of the teams did not follow a plan but they all participated in the activities imposed by the scenario and switched roles in no certain order. In few cases, the students split tasks and followed the same pattern throughout the whole activity. These teams achieved the minimum knowledge gain on a group level while some members made negative comments for the practice of their fellow students.

The strict structure imposed by the scenario guided the students through the activity. On one hand, the tight planning was necessary due to the nature of the learning objective but on the other hand it did not give students the opportunity to take the initiative, argument and build common knowledge by trial and error. These fundamental characteristics not only allow team members to bond and perform better on a group level. They would also lead to more complicated practices, enriching the user data and thus allowing the application of a bigger set of activity metrics and data analysis methods. In future work, we plan to test different kinds of scenarios with varying degrees of freedom to classroom activities. The concurrent use of multiple devices within a team, the nature of learning activities that could be supported effectively by the use of mobile devices and additional parameters should be further studied in order to fully explore the application of learning analytics for mobile learning collaborative activities.

References

1. Zurita, G., Baloian, N., Baytelman, F.: Using mobile devices to foster social interactions in the classroom. In: 12th International Conference on Computer Supported Cooperative Work in Design, CSCWD 2008, pp. 1041–1046. IEEE (2008)
2. Bollen, L., Giemza, A., Hoppe, H.U.: Flexible analysis of user actions in heterogeneous distributed learning environments. In: Dillenbourg, P., Specht, M. (eds.) EC-TEL 2008. LNCS, vol. 5192, pp. 62–73. Springer, Heidelberg (2008)
3. Ogata, H., Hui, G.L., Yin, C., Ueda, T., Oishi, Y., Yano, Y.: LOCH: supporting mobile language learning outside classrooms. International Journal of Mobile Learning and Organisation (IJMLO) 2(3), 271–282 (2008)
4. Spikol, D., Milrad, M., Maldonado, H., Pea, R.: Integrating co-design practices into the development of mobile science collaboratories. In: Proceedings of the 9th IEEE International Conference on Advanced Learning Technologies (ICALT), Riga, Latvia, pp. 393–397 (2009)
5. Giemza, A., Bollen, L., Hoppe, H.U.: LEMONADE: A flexible authoring tool with support for integrated mobile learning scenarios. International Journal of Mobile Learning and Organisation (IJMLO) 5(1), 96–114 (2010)
6. Verheyen, P., Ziebarth, S., Novak, J., Hoppe, H.U.: Mobile Werkzeuge zur Erstellung multimedialer Notizen als Basis für medizinische Fallbeispiele. In: Proceedings der Pre-Conference Workshops der 11. e-Learning Fachtagung Informatik-DeLFI 2013. Logos Verlag (2013)

7. Schmitz, B., Ternier, S., Kalz, M., Klemke, R., Specht, M.: Designing a mobile learning game to investigate the impact of role-playing on helping behaviour. In: Hernández-Leo, D., Ley, T., Klamma, R., Harrer, A. (eds.) EC-TEL 2013. LNCS, vol. 8095, pp. 357–370. Springer, Heidelberg (2013)

8. Stenros, J., Waern, A., Montola, M.: Studying the Elusive Experience in Pervasive Games. Simulation & Gaming (2011)

9. Reid, J., Hull, R., Clayton, B., Melamed, T., Stenton, P.: A research methodology for evaluating location aware experiences. Personal Ubiquitous Comput. 15, 53–60 (2011)

10. Aljohani, N.R., Davis, H.C.: Significance of learning analytics in enhancing the mobile and pervasive learning environments. In: 6th International Conference on Next Generation Mobile Applications, Services and Technologies (NGMAST 2012), pp. 70–74. IEEE (2012)

11. Balacheff, N., Lund, K.: Multidisciplinarity vs. Multivocality, the case of learning analytics. In: Proceedings of the Third International Conference on Learning Analytics and Knowledge, pp. 5–13. ACM (2013)

12. Harasim, L.: Collaborating in cyberspace: Using computer conferences as a group learning environment. Interactive Learning Environments 3, 119–130 (1993)

13. Benbunan-Fich, R., Hiltz, S.R.: Impacts of asynchronous learning networks on individual and group problem solving: A field experiment. Group Decision and Negotiation 8, 409–426 (1999)

14. Kahrimanis, G., Chounta, I.A., Avouris, N.: Study of correlations between logfile-based metrics of interaction and the quality of synchronous collaboration. In: 9th International Conference on the Design of Cooperative Systems, Workshop on Analysing the Quality of collaboration, International Reports on Socio-Informatics (IRSI), Aix en Provence, p. 24 (2010)

15. Marshall, P., Hornecker, E., Morris, R., Dalton, S., Rogers, Y.: When the fingers do the talking: A study of group participation for different kinds of shareable surfaces (2008)

16. Hoppe, H.U., Engler, J., Weinbrenner, S.: The Impact of Structural Characteristics of Concept Maps on Automatic Quality Measurement. In: International Conference of the Learning Sciences (ICLS 2012), Sydney, Australia (2012)

17. Schümmer, T., Strijbos, J.W., Berkel, T.: A new direction for log file analysis in CSCL: Experiences with a spatio-temporal metric. In: 2005 Conference on Computer Supported Collaborative Learning (CSCL 2005), pp. 567–576. International Society of the Learning Sciences (2005)

18. Suthers, D.D., Dwyer, N., Medina, R., Vatrapu, R.: A framework for conceptualizing, representing, and analyzing distributed interaction. International Journal of Computer-Supported Collaborative Learning 5, 5–42 (2010)

19. Persico, D., Pozzi, F.: Task, Teams and Time: three Ts to structure CSCL processes. In: Techniques for Fostering Collaboration in Online Learning Communities: Theoretical and Practical Perspectives, pp. 1–14 (2011)

20. Bratitsis, T., Dimitracopoulou, A., Martínez-Monés, A., Marcos, J.A., Dimitriadis, Y.: Supporting members of a learning community using Interaction Analysis tools: The example of the Kaleidoscope NoE scientific network. In: Eighth IEEE International Conference on Advanced Learning Technologies, ICALT 2008, pp. 809–813. IEEE (2008)

21. Sintoris, C., Stoica, A., Papadimitriou, I., Yiannoutsou, N., Komis, V., Avouris, N.: MuseumScrabble: Design of a mobile game for children's interaction with a digitally augmented cultural space. International Journal of Mobile Human Computer Interaction (IJMHCI) 2, 53–71 (2010)

22. Chounta, I.-A., Sintoris, C., Masoura, M., Yiannoutsou, N., Avouris, N.: The good, the bad and the neutral: an analysis of team-gaming activity. In: ECTEL Meets ECSCW 2013: Workshop on Collaborative Technologies for Working and Learning, Cyprus (2013)
23. Ogata, H., Matsuka, Y., El-Bishouty, M.M., Yano, Y.: LORAMS: linking physical objects and videos for capturing and sharing learning experiences towards ubiquitous learning. International Journal of Mobile Learning and Organisation 3(4), 337–350 (2009)
24. Hsu, C.-K., Hwang, G.-J.: A context-aware ubiquitous learning approach for providing instant learning support in personal computer assembly activities. Interactive Learning Environments (2012)
25. Kuenzi, J.J.: Science, technology, engineering, and mathematics (stem) education: Background, federal policy, and legislative action (2008)
26. Giemza, A., Malzahn, N., Hoppe, H.U.: Mobilogue: Creating and conducting mobile learning scenarios in informal settings. In: 21st International Conference on Computers in Education (2013)
27. Gassner, K.: Diskussionen als Szenario zur Ko-Konstruktion von Wissen mit visuellen Sprachen. Universität Duisburg-Essen (2003)
28. Reimann, P.: Time is precious: Variable-and event-centred approaches to process analysis in CSCL research. International Journal of Computer-Supported Collaborative Learning 4, 239–257 (2009)
29. Lou, Y., Abrami, P.C., d'Apollonia, S.: Small group and individual learning with technology: A meta-analysis. Review of Educational Research 71, 449–521 (2001)

Collaborative Search Research
in College Computer Courses

Addison Y.S. Su[1], Chester S.J. Huang[2], T.-J. Ding[3],
Angus F.M. Huang[4], Stephen J.H. Yang[5], and Y.-Z. Hsieh[6]

[1] Advanced Communication Laboratory, National Central University, Taiwan
ncuaddison@gmail.com
[2,5] Department of Computer Science and Information Engineering,
National Central University, Taiwan
shinjia.huang@gmail.com, jhyang@csie.ncu.edu.tw
[3] Department of Electro-Optical and Energy Engineering, MingDao University, Taiwan
tjding@mdu.edu.tw
[4] Institute of Information Science, Academia Sinica, Taiwan
angushuang@iis.sinica.edu.tw
[6] Department of Information Technology and Communication,
Shih-Chien University, Taiwan
yizeng.hsieh@gmail.com

Abstract. The Internet has become the most important information source for students; however, most students lack adequate search processes and search abilities when solving problems using Web search. Current Web search with a single-user environment does not require students to seek assistance in solving their problem. Therefore, how to use information problem solving model to help students solve problems is an emerging issue, and integrated collaborative Web technologies with a suitable model is a key solution. We propose a novel collaborative search system, and it develops the knowledge base of an expert system by organizing the problem of the students. The experimental data were conducted with 36 students at a college school in Northern Taiwan. The results show that collaborative search benefits college student information gathering and improves search processes and search abilities.

Keywords: Collaborative search, Search process, Search ability.

1 Introduction

In recent years, Web search engines have developed significantly, and the proportion of college students using Web search to complete their homework is gradually increasing [1,6]. Web search systems have replaced the library as the major source of information for students. Although students may feel confident when using Web search systems, most students lack basic search processes and search abilities [7,8,9]. Moreover, Web search systems commonly used by students, such as Google, Bing,

T. Yuizono et al. (Eds.): CollabTech 2014, CCIS 460, pp. 143–152, 2014.
© Springer-Verlag Berlin Heidelberg 2014

and Yahoo, are all designed for single users working in an independent environment. With the Web search system architecture, it is difficult for students working in a team to collaborate for seeking information, and students can rely only on their own search experience to solve problems when they encounter difficulties in a single-user Web search activity [4].

Therefore, we propose a novel collaborative search system, named TomoSearch, to elicit and organize knowledge and experiences regarding search strategy from students. TomoSearch is then employed to advise individual students to improve their search processes and search abilities on the Internet. TomoSearch contained functions included in systems of previous studies, such as keyword search, search statistics, and search result reviews. The digital annotation provides a recorded method for students to maintain an information record, and all student thoughts are shared with the whole group to meet awareness requirements. Integrated collaborative search with a proper information solving problem model was applied to a college computer class with 36 students. A series of experimental stages such as the investigation, questionnaire, and discussion revealed how the mechanism benefits the information gathering function of students and improves search processes and search abilities. The aim of this study is to propose the mechanism to improve students' search processes and search abilities. Finally, we explore how to use collaborative search influence students' search processes and search abilities.

2   Collaborative Search

Fig. 1 presents the functions of TomoSearch, which contains search box, group history, search suggestion, digital annotation, and discussion room. Comparison with pervious Web search systems, these functions satisfy college students to divide their search tasks and help each other by communicating and information sharing. When a student logs into the system, he/she can see his/her present collaborators in the group member window on the left side. The group member window shows who is searching for the same task and whether a group member is online or offline. A student can select a group member and talk to him/her using text messaging in the discussion room. The communication function is used to determine the search job, ask for help, or report an information finding. All text messages are kept on the server, enabling offline collaborators to join the discussion room. The group history is sent to their message window when they login.

After a student decides on a search task, he/she easily starts the search using the search box on the top of left. Web search engine choices include Google, Yahoo, and Bing. Different students can use a different Web search engine to expand the search area and reduce the likelihood of everyone finding only the same documents. Search results show in the browser on the right side.

The search processes of the group are aided by keyword suggestions. The system shows the six most frequently used search queries below the search box. Thus, students can learn what search words other members usually use to perform the same or

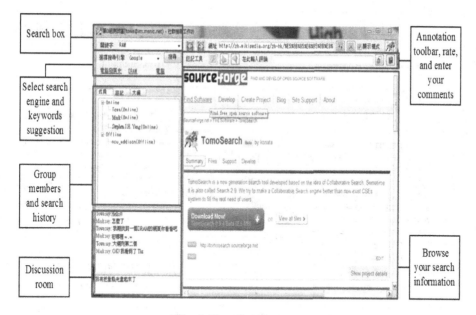

Fig. 1. TomoSearch system

similar search. When he/she clicks a suggested query, the system repeats the search for him/her. The system also tries to auto-complete their typing query using the group search history. Thus, they can more easily pick a suitable search query.

During the browsing process, the digital annotation provides a way for students to keep an information record. These personal and group records can locate information results from their search process. Moreover, the system provides four types of digital annotation to help students record their search results.

a)   Rate: The value of the document. A student can give a positive rating or negative rating (Fig. 2a) to a browsing document based on its usefulness. Based on the rating, users decides whether the document should be suggested to others.

b)   Comment: A short description about the browsed document (Fig. 2b). The description can be used for reminding students of the relationship between the search problem and the document.

c)   Highlight: When a student selects a text block in the browsing window, he/she highlights the selection in yellow (Fig. 2c). This function helps students quickly see the important content in a document and label possible search results.

d)   Relate Document: An advanced function used to keep the relationship between browsing documents. It is like a reference list of documents (Fig. 2d), and students can follow other collaborators' records to find other useful documents quickly.

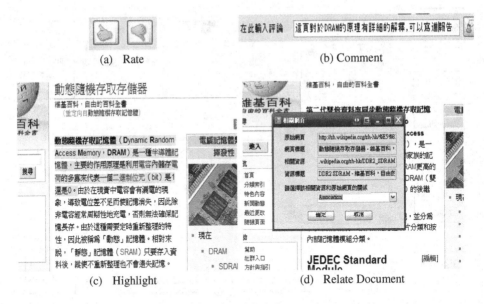

(a) Rate

(b) Comment

(c) Highlight

(d) Relate Document

Fig. 2. Four types of digital annotation

All annotations from each student are shared with the whole group to meet aware-ness requirements. When a student opens a document, the annotation list of the left side shows him/her the entire annotation history that collaborators have made (Fig. 3). If a document contains highlighting, the highlighted text is shown in the browser.

Finally, Students summarize the search processes of collaborators to a teamwork search result summary (Fig. 4). The summary contains all documents students have annotated. The list is ranked according to rating results and the number of highlights; thus, students can quickly find useful documents for the search topic. They can see all search results of the each group member and use the results to finish the task of information processing and organization.

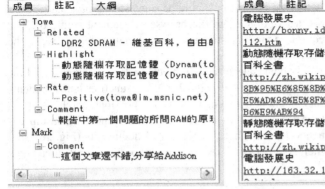

Fig. 3. Annotation list

Fig. 4. Search result summary

3   Methodology

3.1   Participants

This study chose a Taiwan university (17-18 year olds). Thirty-six students (thirty-one male, five female) and one male teacher from a class on Introduction of Computer Science participated in the experiment. Thirty-six students were randomly divided into nine groups, and one teacher from a class on Computer Science participated in the experiment. Researchers have indicated that the number of members in a group could affect students' learning abilities when working in a teamwork environment. Prior studies found that a group consisting of three to six members is appropriate for collaborative learning [2,3,5]. Thus, each group consisted of four members. The teacher periodically assigned students some search problem and asked them to find the answer.

3.2   Experiment Procedure

Students from the selected course met Friday mornings in a computer classroom and focused on Introduction of Computer Science. The course schedule and progress were mainly decided by the teacher. Researchers gave each student a four-page questionnaire for the biographical study.

First, students were instructed to search the problem using a traditional search system, such as Google, Bing, or Yahoo. Each group was assigned a search assignment on Introduction of Computer Science. A search assignment comprised 20 questions that students had to explain. These questions were modified from those used by Tsai and Tsai [10]. Questions were considered knowledge-finding questions, which were evaluated by the teachers based on the correctness, richness, and completeness of the answers. For example, for a search assignment of "computer virus," a group had to find answers to questions like "What is a computer virus?" "How many classifications are computer viruses categorized?" "How do you prevent a computer virus?" A knowledge-finding question requires gathering information and provides a summary regarding relevant knowledge. Students searched for answers on the Internet and were required to record answers in a search diary. At Week 10, students took their group search report and diary as a pre-test.

During Week 11, we introduced the TomoSearch system and gave students one hour to practice using the software. Subsequently, each student was interviewed for five minutes to obtain opinions about the system. Every group was assigned to use the collaborative search system for nine teamwork activities given during Weeks 11 to 19. Each activity was conducted as the assignment. A search assignment comprised 20 questions that students had to explain. These questions also were modified from those used by Tsai and Tsai [10]. A diary and the group search report were handed for each group search assignment. During Week 20, students gave a presentation on their final group teamwork activity. They took their search results, shared reflections, described search processes and the collaborative situation as the post-test. The teacher gave each group a grade based on their presentation, group search report, and post-test.

4   Result and Discussion

One important research question in our study was the influence of collaborative search on students' search processes and search abilities. According to the Information Problem Solving (IPS) model [11], we used the pre-test and post-test to determine the relationship between the five processes of the IPS model. Table 1 shows the means and the standard deviations for the number of search processes were performed by the 36 students. The result indicates a significant difference between the pre-test and post-test in the four processes of search information, scan information, process information, and organizing and presenting information. However, the define problem process had no significant difference between the pre-test and post-test ($t = -1.94$, $p < .05$). The reason is that they already understood that the first sentence of each problem of a topic is critical. Comparisons of the students in search information and scan information processes revealed substantial differences between the pre- and post-tests. A closer observation of the data reveals that the students used more attention between search and scan information processes, meaning that they clicked on a link faster in the traditional search system and, after looking at the website, quickly decided to return to the traditional search system and click on another link. We observed significant differences between the pre- and post-tests for the four processes of "Search information" ($t = 5.68$, $p < .05$), "Scan information" ($t = 6.04$, $p < .05$), "Process information" ($t = -5.29$, $p < .05$), and "Organizing and presenting information" ($t = -2.63$, $p < .05$).

In addition, Fig. 5 shows the time investment in the constituent processes by the 36 students. This result shows that in the post-test student search and scan information reduced more times during the processes. This means that in a collaborative search system, a group can divide and share the search strategy and individual students do not need to comprehend the entire search strategy by himself or herself. Consequently, the result shows that the collaborative search system partially helps students decrease their searching burdens and repeating data sources.

Table 1. Paired-samples t-test for Information Problem Solving (IPS) Model

Item		Mean	N	SD	t	Sig.
Define Problem	Pre-test	2.13	36	0.91	-1.94	0.06
	Post-test	2.63	36	1.21		
Search Information	Pre-test	12.81	36	3.85	5.68	0.00
	Post-test	8.97	36	2.86		
Scan Information	Pre-test	17.59	36	2.95	6.04	0.00
	Post-test	12.91	36	3.55		
Process Information	Pre-test	7.03	36	2.18	-5.29	0.00
	Post-test	11.41	36	3.86		
Organize and Present Information	Pre-test	20.44	36	5.00	-2.63	0.01
	Post-test	24.09	36	5.82		

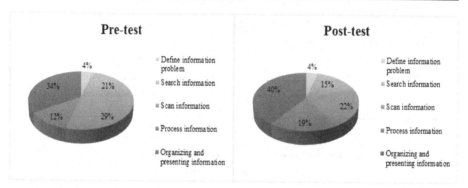

Fig. 5. Representation of difference in time invested in the five processes

Table 2 shows that the results present a significant difference for search abilities between the pre-test and post-test. Furthermore, the typing ability of the post-test was significantly better than that of the pre-test (-9.65, p < .05). The purpose of the test was primarily to examine students' keyword adoption in search processes after using the collaborative search system, that is, the number of keywords adapted than in the post-test compared with the pre-test, after the using collaboration search system. Moreover, the empirical results also revealed a significant difference between the pre- and post-tests.

The clicking ability of the post-test was significantly better than that of the pre-test (-9.70, p < .05). The test was measured by computing the accuracy ratio of the students' clicking documents. When the students searched for information on the Internet, they were required to retrieve and gather information from the searched web documents by using a limited number of words. Thus, the accuracy ratio of clicking documents in the search processes of the corresponding questions was calculated according to the word limit. For the students in the post-test, their usage of keywords and accuracy ratio of clicking documents had both made obvious improvements. They cloud also quickly find accurate answers from just a few web document using important keywords.

Finally, the reading ability of the post-test was significantly better than that of the pre-test (-10.35, p < .05). The purpose of the test was to measure one's efficiency while assessing the first Web site after browsing all the searched documents displayed on the browser. This can act as a reference to understand a student's assessment in determining the first related document. According to the statistics results, the mean of the post-test was higher than that of the pre-test, implying that the students improved their reading ability after employing the collaborative search system. In the process of selecting which document to browse, the students were able to read the description of each candidate document shown on the annotation list and search result summary of the collaborative search system.

Table 2. Paired-samples t-test for search abilities

Item		Mean	N	SD	t	Sig.
Typing	Pre-test	0.40	36	0.14	-9.65	0.00
	Post-test	0.70	36	0.14		
Clicking	Pre-test	0.40	36	0.13	-9.70	0.00
	Post-test	0.67	36	0.10		
Reading	Pre-test	0.47	36	0.11	-10.35	0.00
	Post-test	0.74	36	0.11		
Average Score	Pre-test	0.42	36	0.09	-13.70	0.00
	Post-test	0.70	36	0.08		

5   Conclusion

This study examined the influence of collaborative search on students' search processes and abilities. We explored the information background of students and let them search the Internet as a group in two different ways. One way was using traditional search; the other was using collaborative search. We observed the difference between the two kinds of activities to determine the influence of the collaborative search system on search processes and search abilities. Experimental results indicate that collaborative search improves the search processes of students and raises search abilities. Collaborative search encourages students to learn better search strategy from their collaborators and revise their own search processes. Unfortunately, although collaborative search provides a good way for students to solve their information problems, it is unsuitable for all students. Our experiment result revealed that some students with low information background tend to avoid collaborating with group members via the Internet. The extra search tool steps become a barrier in their search process.

This study determined the influence of a collaborative search system on information problem solving activities of students and showed that the system helps students improve their search skills each other. Future research should be expanded to investigate the influence of a collaborative search system on students with various educational backgrounds, locations, and learning styles.

Acknowledgements. Our work was funded by Ministry of Education Republic of Taiwan and Ministry of Science and Technology of Taiwan. And this research was funded by "Research Center for Advanced Science and Technology Project" at National Central University of Taiwan.

References

1. Cromley, G.J., Azevedo, R.: Locating Information within Extended Hypermedia. Educational Technology Research and Development 57(3), 287–313 (2009)
2. Dillenbourg, P.: Collaborative Learning. Cognitive and Computational Approaches. Pergamon, Amsterdam (1999)
3. Gros, B.: Instructional Design for Computer-Supported Collaborative Learning in Primary and Secondary School. Computer in Human Behavior 17, 173–190 (2011)
4. Hansen, P., Järvelin, K.: Collaborative Information Retrieval in an Information-Intensive Domain. Information Processing & Management 41(2), 1101–1119 (2005)
5. Johnson, D.W., Johnson, R.T., Smith, K.A.: Cooperative Learning Returns to College: What Evidence is There that it Works? Change 30(4), 26–35 (1998)
6. Kuiper, E., Volman, M., Terwel, J.: The Web as an Information Resource in K-12 Education: Strategies for Supporting Students in Searching and Processing Information. Review of Education Research 75(3), 285–328 (2005)
7. Pritchard, A., Cartwright, V.: Transforming that they Read: Helping Eleven-Year-Olds Engage with Internet information. Literacy 38(1), 26–31 (2004)

8. Schacter, J., Chung, G.K.W.K., Dorr, A.: Children's Internet Searching on Complex Problems: Performance and Process Analysis. Journal of the American Society for Information Science 49(9), 840–849 (1998)

9. Shenton, A.K., Dixon, P.: A Comparison of Youngsters' Use of CD-ROM and the Internet as Information Resources. Journal of the American Society for Information Science and Technology 54(11), 1029–1049 (2003)

10. Tsai, M.J., Tsai, C.C.: Information Searching Strategies in Web-Based Science Learning: The Role of Internet Self-Efficacy. Innovations in Education and Teaching International 40(1), 43–50 (2003)

11. Walraven, A., Brand-Gruwel, S., Boshuizen, H.P.A.: How Students Evaluate Information and Sources When Searching the World Wide Web for Information. Computers & Education 52(1), 234–246 (2009)

TUtor Collaborator Using Multi-Agent System

Márcio Alencar and José Francisco Netto

Post-Graduate Program in Computer Science (PPGI),
Federal University of Amazonas (UFAM), Manaus, AM, Brazil
{marcio.alencar,jnetto}@icomp.ufam.edu.br

Abstract. A common problem in Virtual Learning Environments is the difficult task to monitor students activities and the lack of feedback from the tutor. Use of new technologies to perform the tracking of students in virtual environments can bring great results, facilitating the work students and teachers This paper presents TUCUMÃ, an 3D Intelligent Virtual Agent integrated into an Environment Virtual Learning Moodle. It works as a distance learning course tutor, monitoring students activities, removing doubts of the students through dialog. The avatar is composed of MultiAgent System responsible for producing gestures and monitoring students activities.

Keywords: VLE, Multi-Agent System, Embodied Conversational Agent, Affective Computing, AIML, Moodle.

1   Introduction

It is growing number of Worldwide educational institutions using Virtual Learning Environments (VLE) such as educational support tool for students. Among the various VLEs can highlight Moodle, used in over 200 countries. In these environments students and teachers can interact, exchanging information and experiences.

Research [1] shows that follow up of students in distance learning courses is quite a tiresome task and requires much time from the tutor. It is essential that the tutor and the students learn to monitor, as reflected in its formation and consequently the success of the course.

An activity widely used in VLEs is the forum because there is better collaboration, as participants use communication (messages exchange), cooperation (operate on the same shared space) and coordination (organize) [2]. However, tutors spend a good part of his time reading the forum posts and checking students' participation. Another time consuming activity is the tracking of the tasks sent to a repository, because they have deadlines.

The lack of tools in Moodle to assist in monitoring activities, motivated this research, where we propose the developed of a prototype of 3D avatar, which uses Multi-Agent System (MAS) acting in VLE Moodle using AIML (Artificial Intelligence Markup Language) and framework JADE (Java Agent Development Framework). TUCUMÃ (TUtor Collaborator Using MultiAgent system) is responsible for performing the monitoring of students' activities, stating that activities are pending or days,

T. Yuizono et al. (Eds.): CollabTech 2014, CCIS 460, pp. 153–159, 2014.

and ask questions about the discipline through a dialogue, where the student will listen to the answers of the 3D virtual tutor and track body movements issued by the avatar.

2   Multi-Agent Systems

A Multi-Agent System (MAS) is a type of distributed Artificial Intelligence system composed by agents that act (sensors and actuators) in an environment, interacting, negotiating and coordinating actions to solve problems. Agents with behaviors, each with a different function and through interactions with the environments can produce excellent results [3].

In order to contribute to our research, we can mention the work of researchers [4] who developed ARARA (Artifacts and Requirements Awareness Reinforcement Agents), a collaborative tool that assists members in the software development process. This SMA performs monitoring the team members, even distant geographically, detecting and notifying changes in the project. MetaTutor [5] is a hypermedia learning environment, which talks about the human circulatory system. It consists of four pedagogical agents that guide, monitor, establish dialogue and provide feedback to students using natural language. RITS (Remote Intelligent Tutoring System) [6] is an environment for interactive learning developed in Java and ASP, which helps teachers and students. RITS has a SMA that works as a tutor, answering questions from students and performing tracking tasks. The researchers [7] have developed a new system of distance learning in 3D, entitled GE3D. It is a virtual campus, produced with the SCOL technology using ITS (Intelligent Tutoring System) to track pupils with difficulties in VLE. Quizmaster [8] is an intelligent collaborative assessment tool inserted in a 3D virtual game where each student is represented by an avatar. Pupil participation is made through a Quiz, where they are evaluated by their responses. TQ- Bot [9] is a chatterbot integrated in VLE, representing the figure of the tutor, talking and solving doubts of students. Researchers [10] created the chatterbot CHARLIE (Chatter Learning Interface Entity) and EMMA (Agent Manager Events and Messages) and ISMAEL Agents (Intelligent System Manager Agent for E- Learning), that perform monitoring of students by providing a personalized education and efficient.

3   Embodied Conversational Agents (ECAs)

The use of Embodied Conversational Agents (ECAs) in VLEs are critical, as they help students learning through better interaction and motivation [11].Such agents can observe the behavior of the students, checking their emotions .

Among the several studies we highlight the work of [12] which describes Guru, an animated tutor agent in 3D, talking about more than 120 subjects in biology, with high school students. PAT2Math multimedia [13] is an intelligent tutor that helps students in solving algebra equations and elementary school, while the agent Help Tutor [14] is an integrated intelligent agent to geometry Cognitive Tutor commercial software to assist in learning geometry. Divalite [15] is a framework for integrating animated conversational agent on web pages. Greta [16] is a 3D virtual agent, able to speak through a communication using gestures, gaze and head movement. Gaze Tutor [17] was developed to accompany students on a biology course through eye tracking, checking students who are bored or off course, it uses dialogue to return the students to school. EMASPEL [18] is a framework endowed with cognitive and affective capable of analyzing facial expressions during class to get information about the student agents , in order to increase motivation of students, encouraging learning.

4   Affective Computing

The Affective Computing is the area of computing related with emotional aspects [19]. Several Affective Computing scientists are interested in put the animated pedagogical agents into VLE, capable of interacting with users in more anthropomorphic way through gestures and emotional facial expressions [20]. Studies show that pedagogical agents can increase communication skills, as well as attract the user's attention with gestures, assisting students in the teaching-learning process. According to [19], for computers being intelligent it is necessary improve interaction with humans, recognizing and expressing emotions. We can see positive results with the use of emotions in work [21] that shows that there is a difference between a dialogue with the user using only text and dialogue using ECAs.

5   Employed Technologies

The TUCUMÃ avatar was developed with technology ALICE (Artificial Linguistic Internet Computer Entity), which uses the AIML interpreter that uses AIML language. AIML (Artificial Intelligence Markup Language) is an open source language based on XML, where questions and answers are written forming the chatbot knowledge base [22]. The avatar needs an AIML interpreter, that uses Natural Processing language, to answer questions of users [23].   AIML interpreter used in this project was the program-O [24], which uses the PHP programming language and database MySQL intelligent agents used in monitoring the activities and movements of the avatar, were implemented with JADE. We will use the Moodle (Modular Object-Oriented Dynamic Learning Environment). 3D avatar and your moviments can be seen in the Moodle through the software Haptek Player, which uses JavaScript code. We used the synthesizer Windows Speech, TTS (Text to Speech) to speak the responses issued by avatar, similar technologies have been used in research [25]. It was installed a Brazilian Portuguese male voice of Felipe, produced by the company Loquendo. While the web system, in charge of generating the AIML files automatically, will be developed in language programming PHP using MySQL database.

6   Prototype

Figure 1 shows the architecture of TUCUMÃ, composed of the main elements: tutor, student, Moodle, TUCUMÃ Intelligent Virtual Agent, the agents responsible for the gesture of the avatar and agents responsible for monitoring the activities of the Virtual Learning Environment.

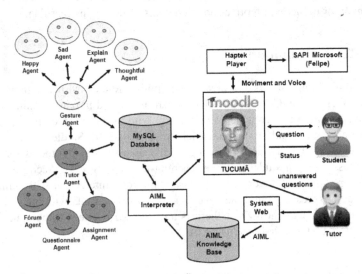

Fig. 1. TUCUMÃ Architecture

This architecture is in development and to better understand, we explain your functioning in detail hereafter.

The tutor responsible for the course or discipline will register questions and answers about the course which is responsible, using SisAIML, a web system. The SisAIML will receive the data registered by the Tutor and then generate an AIML file, identified with the name of discipline, then the SisAIML will generate variations of questions and answers indexed so that the dialogue between the avatar and the student does not become monotonous. This file will compose Knowledge-based TUCUMÃ Agent. The AIML interpreter will read the file generated by SisAIML.

Students when entering the distance learning course, will see the avatar on the right side of the screen and can ask questions about the discipline to avatar, as well as know their situation on the course. If the student wishes to put a question to TUCUMÃ, the same with the help of AIML interpreter will look for the answer in his knowledge base and return the response. For this to happen the Tutor Agent will inform the Gesture Agent, which will examine the question of the student. If the question has answer then the Gesture Agent will communicate with Explain Agent, who performs movements in the arms of characterizing avatar that is explaining the answer. Otherwise the agent will gesture will communicate with the Thoughtful Agent, which will perform nod Avatar, featuring not know the answer, but it talks to the student that will send your question to the distance tutor (unanswered questions), then the Tutor Agent that sends a message inside the AVA to tutor the distance tutor (unanswered questions), then the Tutor Agent that sends a message inside the AVA to distance tutor.

If the student wants to know your situation on the course, will click on the status button, it will query the avatar Tutor Agent, which will communicate with agents responsible for the activities: Forum, Assignment and Questionnaire. The Forum Agent is responsible for informing the student's participation in the forum. Questionnaire Agent is responsible for informing if the student made the questionnaire and Assignment Agent is responsible for informing if the student sent his activity. With that the three agents will report the status of its activities to Agent Tutor that will generate a contextual response and inform the user how is your situation on the course in real time. When the TUCUMÃ Agent verifies that the student is with their current activities, then it will express happiness, congratulate the student and clap (happy). If the student is late with activities, then the avatar will put his hand on face (sad). If the avatar knows the answer of the question, then it will open of the arms (explaining) and if he certainly do not know, he will put the chin hand (thinking), as can be seen in Figure 2.

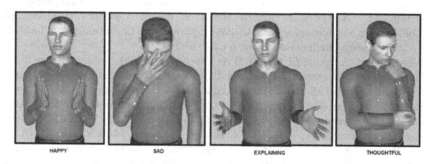

Fig. 2. Gestures of the TUCUMÃ

We believe that the gestures produced by avatar during the dialogue with the student can help in a better understanding of the topic addressed. Facial gestures issued expressed by ECA were presented in software HapFACS, a tool that enables you to view the avatar emotions: angry, contempt, disgust, embarrassment, fear, happiness, pride, sadness and surprise [26].

7   Discussion and Future Work

This paper presented the development of a TUCUMÃ intelligent agent that is integrated with Moodle Virtual Learning Environment in order to monitor the activities of students in distance learning courses, as well as answer questions about the course. Our research project is under development, we intend to improve the avatar gestures, conduct experiments with class of students of the institution. We also intend to create new intelligent agents that will monitor other activities.

We believe the use of intelligent agents provides more security and motivation to students, such as their interaction through dialogues, which can draw the student's attention when needed and praise when days with activities. The avatar symbolizes the course tutor, and these actions can avoid isolation, disinterest and evasion course, moreover think emotions it might stimulate students, in order to motivate students to perform tasks and stay on course.

Acknowledgements. The authors are grateful to Foundation for Research Support of the State of Amazonas (FAPEAM) and Federal University of Amazonas (UFAM) for the financial support given to this research.

References

1. Alencar, M. A. S.; Netto, J.F.M. (2011) Improving cooperation in Virtual Learning Environments using multi-agent systems and AIML. FIE, pp.F4C-1-F4C-6, 2011 Frontiers in Education Conference, 2011.
2. Steinmacher, I.; Chaves, A. & Gerosa, M. (2010). Awareness Support in Global Software Development: A Systematic Review Based on the 3C Collaboration Model, ed., 'Collaboration and Technology 16th CRIWG Conference on Collaboration and Technology, 2010', Springer Berlin / Heidelberg, pp. 185-201.
3. Alencar, M. A. S.; Netto, J.F.M. (2012) An Experiment with Multi-Agent System in Virtual Learning Environment. In T. Amiel & B. Wilson (Eds.), Proceedings of World Conference on Educational Multimedia, Hypermedia and Telecommunications, p. 2791-2798.
4. Ester J. C. de Lima, José A. Rodrigues Nt., Geraldo Xexéo, Jano Moreira de Souza (2010) ARARA - A collaborative tool to requirement change awarenes. CSCWD 2010: 134-139
5. Azevedo, R., Johnson, A., Burkett, C., Chauncey, A., Lintean, M., & Rus, V. (2010). The role of prompting and feedback in facilitating students' learning about science with Meta-Tutor. Proceedings of the Twenty-fourth AAAI Conference on Artificial Intelligence, Atlanta, GA.
6. Yi, Z., Zhao, K., Li, Y., Cheng, P. (2010) Remote Intelligent Tutoring System Based on Multi-Agent. In: Proceedings of The 2nd International Conference on Information Engineering and Computer Science, Wuhan, China, vol. 3, pp. 958–961, 2010
7. Jean Grieu, Florence Lecroq, Patrick Person, Thierry Galinho, Hadhoum Boukachour (2010) GE3D: A Virtual Campus for Technology-Enhanced Distance Learning. iJET 5(3): 12-17
8. Sima Shabani, Fuhua Lin, and Sabine Graf (2012). A Framework for User Modeling in QuizMASter. Invited Paper. Journal of e-Learning and Knowledge Society, Vol. 8, No 3, pp. 29-44.
9. Rodríguez, M. C. ; Fontenla, J. F, A. Mikic Fonte, Perez, R; Martín; Nistal, L. Villavencio, J.C. (2011) A SOA-based Middleware to Integrate Chatterbots in e-Learning Systems. Congresso Iberoamericano de Telemática (CITA 2011), Proceedings,ISSN 1519-132X
10. Fernando A. Mikic Fonte, Juan C. Burguillo, Martín Llamas Nistal. (2012) An intelligent tutoring module controlled by BDI agents for an e-learning platform. Expert Systems with Applications 39 (8), pp. 7546-7554. 2012.
11. Yugo Hayashi, Koya Ono. (2013) Embodied conversational agents as peer collaborators: Effects of multiplicity and modality. RO-MAN 2013: 120-125

12. Olney, A., D'Mello, S. K., Person, N., Cade, W., Hays, P., Williams, C., Lehman, B., & Graesser, A. C. (2012). Guru: A Computer Tutor that Models Expert Human Tutors. In S. Cerri, W. Clancey, G. Papadourakis, & K. Panourgia (Eds.) Proceedings of the 11th International Conference on Intelligent Tutoring Systems (pp. 256-261).

13. Jaques, P. ; Seffrin, H. ; Rubi, G. ; Morais, F. ; Guilardi, C. ; Bittencourt, I. I. ; Isotani, Seiji. (2013) Rule-based expert systems to support step-by-step guidance in algebraic problem solving: The case of the tutor PAT2Math. Expert Systems with Applications. v. 40, p. 5456-5465, 2013.

14. Roll, I., Aleven, V., McLaren, B.M., & Koedinger, K.R. (2011). Improving students' help-seeking skills using metacognitive feedback in an intelligent tutoring system. Learning and Instruction, 21, 267-280.

15. Sansonnet, j.; Correa, d.; Jaques, p ; Braffort, a. ; Verrecchia, c. (2012) Developing Web fully-integrated conversational assistant agents. In: ACM Research in Applied Computation Symposium (RACS), 2012, Texas. p. 14-19.

16. Rajagopal, M. K.; Horain, P. & Pelachaud, C. (2011). Virtually Cloning Real Human with Motion Style., in Milos Kudelka; Jaroslav Pokorný; Václav Snásel & Ajith Abraham, ed., 'IHCI' , Springer, , pp. 125-136 .

17. Sidney K. D'Mello, Andrew Olney, Claire Williams, Patrick Hays. (2012) Gaze tutor: A gaze-reactive intelligent tutoring system. Int. J. Hum.-Comput. Stud. 377-398

18. Mohamed Ben Ammar, Mahmoud Neji, Adel M. Alimi, Guy Gouardères. (2010) The Affective Tutoring System. Expert Syst. Appl. 37(4): 3013-3023

19. R.W. Picard (2003). Affective Computing: Challenges. International Journal of Human-Computer Studies, Volume 59, Issues 1-2, July 2003, pp. 55-64.

20. Margaux Lhommet and Stacy Marsella. (2013) Gesture with Meaning, in Intelligent Virtual Agents, Aug. 2013.

21. Christine L. Lisetti, Reza Amini, Ugan Yasavur, Naphtali Rishe. (2013) I Can Help You Change! An Empathic Virtual Agent Delivers Behavior Change Health Interventions. ACM Trans. Management Inf. Syst. 4(4): 19 (2013)

22. Mikic, F. A., Burguillo, J. C., Llamas, M., Rodríguez, D. A., Rodríguez, E. (2009). CHARLIE: An AIML-based chatterbot which works as an interface among INES and humans, 20th European Association for Education in Electrical and Information Engineering – EAEEIE 2009 (Valencia, Spain), 2009

23. Olney, A. M., Graesser, A. C., & Person, N. K. (2010). Tutorial Dialog in Natural Language. In R. Nkambou, J. Bourdeau, & R. Mizoguchi (Eds.), Advances in Intelligent Tutoring Systems, Studies in Computational Intelligence (Vol. 308, pp. 181-206). Berlin: Springer-Verlag.

24. Jianming Liu, and Steven L. Grant (2012) MMDAvatar - An Online Voice Chat Robot with 3D Avatar and Artificial Intelligence. ASEE Midwest Sect 2012 Annual Conference.

25. Alencar, M. A. S.; Netto, J. F.M. (2011). Developing a 3D Conversation Agent Talking About Online Courses. In T. Bastiaens & M. Ebner (Eds.), Proceedings of World Conference on Educational Multimedia, Hypermedia and Telecommunications 2011 (pp. 1713-1719). Chesapeake, VA: AACE.

26. Reza Amini, Christine L. Lisetti. (2013) HapFACS: An Open Source API/Software to Generate FACS-Based Expressions for ECAs Animation and for Corpus Generation. In 2013 Humaine Association Conference on Affective Computing and Intelligent Interaction, ACII 2013, Geneva, Switzerland, September 2-5, pages 270-275, IEEE, 2013

Author Index